W9-AUD-967

MELISENDE
OF
JERUSALEM

*The World of a Forgotten
Crusader Queen*

MARGARET TRANOVICH

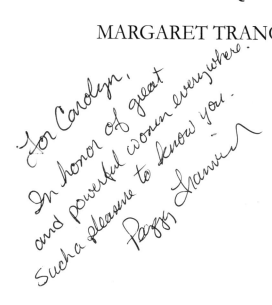

For Carolyn,
In honor of great
and powerful women everywhere.
Such a pleasure to know you.
Peggy Tranovich

EAST & WEST
PUBLISHING

LONDON

© Margaret Tranovich, 2011

The right of Margaret Tranovich to be identified as the author of this work has
been asserted by her in accordance with the Copyright, Designs
and Patents Act 1988.

All rights reserved. No part of this work, its text or any or part of the illustrations
and drawings, may be reproduced, stored in a retrieval system, or transmitted in
any form or by any means, electronic, mechanical, photocopying, recording or
otherwise, without the prior permission of the copyright owner.

Melisende of Jerusalem
The World of
a Forgotten Crusader Queen
First published 2011 by
EAST & WEST PUBLISHING LIMITED
London
ISBN 978 1 907318 06 1

www.eastandwestpublishing.com

Produced by Melisende UK Limited
Printed and bound in Malta at the Gutenberg Press

for
James and Anja

CONTENTS

MAPS, PLATES AND PHOTO CREDITS

MAPS

THE PLATES AND PHOTO CREDITS

(Plates in black and white are indicated by an asterisk)

1.1 Front cover, Queen Melisende Psalter, ivory, c. 1135. (© The British Library Board, Ms. Egerton 1139)

1.2 Queen Melisende Psalter, front cover, ivory, details. (© The British Library Board, Ms. Egerton 1139)

2.1 St John's College, Cambridge, MS B.20 f.2v, detail. Detail showing the signs of the Zodiac and labours of the months for September to December. From f.2v of MS B.20. English, 12th century. September: Libra; vintaging October: Scorpio; sowing November: Sagittarius; killing hogs December: Capricorn; gathering wood. (By permission of the Master and Fellows of St John's College, Cambridge)

2.2 Exterior, St Sernin, Toulouse, France, 1080-1117. (© Holly Hayes/Art History Images)*

2.3 Nave, St Sernin, Toulouse, France, 1080-1117. (© Ian Dagnall/Alamy)*

2.4 Church of St Lazare, Autun, France, by Gislebertus, 1120-1140. (© David Keith Jones/Alamy)*

2.4a Detail of 2.4, door of Church of St Lazare, Autun, Gislebertus, 1120-1140. (© David Keith Jones/Alamy)*

2.5 Winchester Psalter, 1121-1161. (© The British Library Board, Cotton Nero C.iv, f 39)

2.6 Map of Jerusalem, France, c. 1200. (Koninklijke Bibliotheek, The Hague)

2.7 Crusaders besieging Nicaea, MS Français 2630 fol. 22v, Bibliothèque National, Paris. (© The Art Gallery Collection/Alamy)

3.1 St. Michael, Queen Melisende Psalter, 1135, folio 205. (© The British Library Board, Ms. Egerton 1139)

3.2 Mosaic lunette over the doorway into the inner narthex of Hagia Sophia. (© N Reed of QEDImages/Alamy)

3.3   John II Comnenus, Byzantine Emperor (1118-1143). Detail of the mosaic 'Madonna flanked by John Comnenus and his wife the Empress Irene'. Byzantine, c.1118-22. Istanbul, Hagia Sophia, south gallery. (Photo: akg-images/Erich Lessing)

3.4   Gold *hyperpyron* of Alexius I Comnenus, Byzantine, 1092-1118. (Courtesy of the American Numismatic Society)*

3.5   Hagia Sophia, Istanbul, Turkey, 532-537. (© JLImages/Alamy)*

3.6   Interior, Hagia Sophia. (© Walter B Denny)*

3.7   Christ Pantocrator. Dome mosaic, late 11th century, Church of the Monastery at Daphni, Greece. (© INTERFOTO/Alamy)

3.8   Enamel with precious stones; half-length figure of the Archangel Michael. Venice, St Mark's Basilica (Treasury). (© 2011.Photo Scala, Florence)

3.9   The J Paul Getty Museum, Los Angeles, Ms. Ludwig II 4, fol. 106v. Artist unknown, Saint John the Evangelist, 1133, Tempera colours, gold leaf, gold paint, and ink on parchment, Leaf: 22.1 x 18.1 cm ($8^{11}/_{16}$ x $7^{1}/_{8}$ in.)

3.10 Pendant Icon with Christ with the Book blessing (front) and the Virgin Orans (back), Byzantine, first half of 12th century. (Former Trésor de l'abbaye de Saint-Denis MR95. Photo: © RMN/Daniel Arnaudet/Paris, musée du Louvre)

3.11 Textile. Spain, 11th-12th century. Silk compound twill. 51.2 x 32.6 cm ($20^{3}/_{16}$ x $12^{13}/_{16}$ in.). (Gift of John Pierpont Morgan, 1902-1-222. Photo: Scott Hyde. © 2011. Cooper-Hewitt, National Design Museum, Smithsonian Institution/Art Resource, NY/Scala, Florence)

3.12 Incense burner in the shape of a domed building, Byzantine, 12th century. (© 2011. Photo Scala, Florence)*

3.13 Temple pendant and stick, late 11th-first half of 12th century. (New York, Metropolitan Museum of Art. Cloisonné enamel, gold. Rogers Fund, 1990. Acc.n.: 1990.235a, b. © 2011. Image copyright The Metropolitan Museum of Art/Art Resource/Scala, Florence)

3.14 Bowl with griffin attacking a doe, Byzantine, 12th century. (© Dumbarton Oaks, Byzantine Collection, Washington, DC)*

3.15 The outer container of a reliquary of the True Cross one of the richest and most elaborate ensembles of Byzantine enamels to have survived the sack of Constantinople in 1204. Byzantine, c. 955. Constantinople. Silver-gilt and enamel. (Werner Forman Archive/ Cathedral Treasury, Limburg, Germany)

4.1   The Dome of the Rock, Jerusalem, 691. (© Ryan Rodrick Beiler/Alamy)

4.2   Interior, Dome of the Rock. (© Hanan Isachar/Alamy)

4.3   Interior, Dome of the Rock. (© www.BibleLandPictures.com/Alamy)

4.4   Mosaics and Arabic inscriptions, interior, Dome of the Rock. (B O'Kane/Alamy)

4.5   Courtyard, Great Mosque of Damascus, 706. (Photo: author)

4.6   Mosaics on exterior of prayer hall, Great Mosque of Damascus, 706. (Photo: author)

4.7   Qibla wall with *mihrab* and *minbar*, Sultan Hasan madrasa-mausoleum-mosque, Cairo, Egypt, 1356-1363. (© B O'Kane/Alamy)*

4.8   Bowl with kufic script, Samarkand, 11-12th c. (AA96 © RMN/Thierry Ollivier/Paris, musée du Louvre)*

4.9   Jug, Iran, 12th century. (Ashmolean Museum, University of Oxford)

4.10 Bowl with Eagle, Fatimid, c. 1000. (Gift of Mr and Mrs Charles K Wilkinson, 1963. Inv.63.178.1 © 2011. Image copyright The Metropolitan Museum of Art/Art Resource/Scala, Florence)

4.11 Bottle. Probably Iran, about 12th century. Translucent deep green glass; mold-blown with applied decoration. H. 25.8 cm. (Collection of The Corning Museum of Glass, Corning, NY (55.1.6))

4.12 Sprinkler. Near East, possibly 12th to 13th centuries. Transparent colourless glass with greenish tinge; blown. H. 21.3 cm. (Collection of The Corning Museum of Glass, Corning, NY, gift of I C Elston, Jr. (54.1.73))

4.13 Silver sprinkler with cap, early 12th century. (Freer Gallery of Art, Smithsonian Institution, Washington, DC: Purchase, F1950.5)*

4.14 St Josse silk, Khurasan, before 960. (OA7502 © RMN/Hervé Lewandowski/ Paris, musée du Louvre)

4.15 A leaf from a Qu'ran with gold kufic script on blue parchment, Kairouan, Tunisia. 9th century. (Werner Forman Archive/Mrs Bashir Mohamed Collection)

4.16 Fatimid ivory plaque, 11th-12th c. (bpk/Museum für Islamische Kunst, Staatliche Museen zu Berlin/Georg Niedermeiser)*

4.17 Cauldron. Made by Muhammad ibn ʿAbd al-Wahid and Masʿud ibn Ahmad al-Naqqash. Iran, Herat. 12th-early 13th century. Bronze (brass), silver and copper; cast, forged and decorated with inlay. H. 18.5 cm. (Inv.no. IR-2268. The State Hermitage Museum, St Petersburg. Photograph © The State Hermitage Museum/photo by Vladimir Terebenin, Leonard Kheifets, Yuri Molodkovets)

4.17a Cauldron (detail). Made by Muhammad ibn ʿAbd al-Wahid and Masʿud ibn Ahmad al-Naqqash. Iran, Herat. 12th-early 13th century. Bronze (brass), silver and copper; cast, forged and decorated with inlay. H. 18.5 cm. (Inv.no. IR-2268. The State Hermitage Museum, St Petersburg. Photograph © The State Hermitage Museum/photo by Vladimir Terebenin, Leonard Kheifets, Yuri Molodkovets)

4.18 Inlaid silver spoon and fork, front and back. Iran, 12th century. (© The al-Sabah Collection, Dar al-Athar al-Islamiyyah, Kuwait)*

4.19 Banquet scene from the *Maqamat* of al-Hariri, 11th c. (Ms Arabe 5847,fol. 47b, Bibliothèque nationale de France)

5.1 Plan of the Church of the Holy Sepulchre. (after Folda)*

5.2 South transept entrance to the Church of the Holy Sepulchre, Jerusalem, 1149. (École Biblique)*

5.3 Church of the Holy Sepulchre, western lintel, The Last Supper (after Folda)*

5.4 Western lintel, Raising of Lazarus (after Folda)*

5.5 Eastern lintel, detail (after Folda)*

5.6 Eastern lintel, detail (after Folda)*

5.7 Back of eastern lintel, Fatimid sculpture (after Folda)*

5.8 View of Church of Holy Sepulchre from neighbouring rooftop. (Dr John Crook, Winchester)

5.9 Church of the Holy Sepulchre, capitals of transept façade. (Photo: author)*

5.10 Church of the Holy Sepulchre, moulding of transept façade. (Photo: author)*

5.11 Church of the Holy Sepulchre, view to main portal. (Dr John Crook, Winchester)*

5.12 Church of the Holy Sepulchre, view to choir vault and apse from dome. (Dr John Crook, Winchester)*

5.13 *Deesis*, Queen Melisende Psalter, c. 1135, folio 12v. (© The British Library Board, Ms. Egerton 1139)

5.14 *Incipit* page, *Beatus Vir*, folio 23v, Queen Melisende Psalter, c. 1139.(© The

British Library Board, Ms. Egerton 1139)

5.15 Reliquary of the True Cross from Denkendorf, front and back, Jerusalem, c. 1130 (rock crystal mount probably not original). (Photos: P Frankenstein, H Zwietasch; Landesmuseum Württemberg, Stuttgart)*

5.16 Lustre-painted ceramic bowl with lion, Egypt, 12th century. (© The al-Sabah Collection, Dar al-Athar al-Islamiyyah, Kuwait)

5.17 Gold wine bowl, Iran, 11th century. (© The Trustees of the British Museum. All rights reserved)

5.18 Perfume Sprinkler *(Qumqum)*. Probably Syria; 11th-mid-13th century. New York, Metropolitan Museum of Art. Glass, greenish; blown, applied blown foot, applied decoration, h. 10¼ in. (26 cm); gr. w. 5¼ in. (13.4 cm). Purchase, Richard S. Perkins Gift, 1977 (1977.164).(© 2011. Image copyright The Metropolitan Museum of Art/Art Resource/Scala, Florence)

5.19 Bowl, Egypt, 11th-12th century. (© The Trustees of the British Museum. All rights reserved)

5.20 Beaker, Syria, 12-13th c. (© The al-Sabah Collection, Dar al-Athar al-Islamiyyah, Kuwait)

5.21 Carved rock crystal chess pieces, Fatimid, probably Egypt. (© The al-Sabah Collection, Dar al-Athar al-Islamiyyah, Kuwait)*

5.22 Bottle. Near East, Syria, or Egypt, Islamic, probably 10th to 12th century. Deep blue and opaque white glass; blown and tooled. H. 14.7 cm. (Collection of The Corning Museum of Glass, Corning, NY (50.1.32))

5.23 Cope with peacock motif and kufic inscription (silk embroidery) by Islamic School, 11-12th c., St. Sernin, Toulouse, France. (The Bridgeman Art Library)

6.1 Griffin ewer, Mosan, c. 1150. (© Victoria and Albert Museum, London)

6.2 Lion aquamanile, 1200-1250, German, Lower Saxony (© Victoria and Albert Museum, London)*

6.3 The J Paul Getty Museum, Los Angeles, Ms. Ludwig II 4, fol. 69v. Artist unknown, Saint Luke, 1133, Tempera colours, gold leaf, gold paint, and ink on parchment, Leaf: 22.1 x 18.1 cm (8^{11}/$_{16}$ x 7^{1}/$_{8}$ in.).

6.4 The J Paul Getty Museum, Los Angeles, Ms. 4, leaf 1. Artist unknown, The Annunciation, about 1240. Tempera colours, gold leaf, and iron gall ink on parchment, Leaf: 17.8 x 13.5 cm (7 x 5^{5}/$_{16}$ in.).

6.5 The J Paul Getty Museum, Los Angeles. Artist Simone Martini Lippo Vanni, St Luke, 1330s. Tempera and gold leaf on panel, unframed: 56.5 x 36.8 cm (22¼ x 14½ in.) Framed (with original engaged frame): 67.5 x 48.3 cm (26^{9}/$_{16}$ x 19 in.).

6.6 Bronze horses of San Marco, Venice. (© Tibor Bognar/Alamy)*

6.7 Nave of San Marco, Venice. (© John Elk III/Alamy)

6.8 Portion of Pala d'Oro, San Marco, Venice. (© 2011. Cameraphoto/Scala, Florence)

6.9 Andrea del Verrocchio, *David*, c. 1473-75. (Bargello National Museum, Florence. Mary Evans Picture Library. Raffaello Bencini/Alinari Archives, Florence—reproduced with the permission of Ministero per i Ben)*

6.10 Gentile de Fabriano, Madonna and Child, c. 1422. (Pisa, Museo Nazionale di San Matteo. © 2011. Photo Scala, Florence—courtesy of the Ministero Beni e Att. Culturali)

6.11 Brass tray inlaid with silver and gold, Cairo or Damascus, 1345-6. (© The Trustees of the British Museum. All rights reserved)

6.12 Dish, Iran, 9-10th c.; St Mark's Basilica (Treasury) Venice. Relief-cut glass;

mount: gilded silver with cloisonné enamel and precious stones; inv. no. 140; h. 6 cm, d. 7.4 cm. (©2011. Photo Scala, Florence)

6.13 Le Puy Cathedral (Jane Skelding)*

6.14 Dome of the Rock grille, Jerusalem. (Creswell Photographic Archive Ashmolean Museum, neg. EA.CA.4990)*

6.15 Le Puy Cathedral, grille. (Photo: author)*

6.16 Islamic bottle with Christian scenes, Syria, mid-13th c.; H. 28.2 cm, max. diam. 17.8 cm (© Qantara/DMLG. By courtesy of Vaduz, Furusiyya Art Foundation)

6.17 Triptych from Stavelot, c. 1156-58. Byzantine. (New York, The Pierpont Morgan Library. © 2011. Photo Pierpont Morgan Library/Art Resource/ Scala, Florence)

6.18 Trumeau, Souillac, France. (Paul M Maeyaert/age fotostock)*

6.19 Detail, eastern lintel vine scroll from Church of Holy Sepulchre, Jerusalem, 1150 (?). (Collection of the Israel Antiquities Authority)*

6.20 Pisa Baptistry, 1153-1265. (© OJPHOTOS/Alamy)*

6.21 Pisa Griffin, Egypt or Spain (?), 11th century. (Camposanto. © 2011. Photo Scala, Florence)*

6.22 Candlestick, Venice, c. 1550, brass and overlaid with silver. (© Victoria and Albert Museum, London)*

6.23 The Somerset House Conference, 1604 (Juan de Velasco Frias; Juan de Tassis, Count of Villa Mediana; Alessandro Robida; Charles de Ligne, Count of Aremberg; Jean Richardot; Louis Vereyken; Thomas Sackville, Earl of Dorset; Charles Howard, Earl of Nottingham; Charles Blount, Earl of Devonshire; Henry Howard, Earl of Northampton; Robert Cecil, Viscount Cranborne) by unknown artist/oil on canvas, 1604. (© National Portrait Gallery, London)

6.24 Detail of Anatolian carpet in above, 6.24. (© National Portrait Gallery, London)

6.25 Ceiling of the Room of the Horses, Giulio Romano and assistants, c. 1530, Mantua, Palazzo del Te.(© 2011. Photo Scala, Florence)

6.26 Brass jug, Iraq or Iran, 9th century. (© The Trustees of the British Museum. All rights reserved)*

6.27 Glass bowl with base medallion of *senmurv*, Iran, 9-10th century. (© The al-Sabah Collection, Dar al-Athar al-Islamiyyah, Kuwait)*

6.28 Textile fragment with *senmurvs*, Byzantine, 9-10th century. (Photo: Hugo Maertens. © Royal Museums of Art and History, Brussels)

6.29 Textile fragment with *senmurvs*, 11th or 12th century, Eastern Mediterranean. See also col. pl. 3.12. (Gift of John Pierpont Morgan, 1902-1-222. Photo: Scott Hyde © 2011. Cooper-Hewitt, National Design Museum, Smithsonian Institution/Art Resource, NY/Scala, Florence)

ACKNOWLEDGEMENTS

I have been blessed with many powerful, vibrant, and inspiring women in my life. Three of them deserve mention here.

Sahar Huneidi first brought the Psalter of Queen Melisende to my attention and suggested I write about it. That in itself would be enough to merit her inclusion in this section. But thereafter she continued to provide me with encouragement, support, and intellectual stimulation that greatly enhanced the final product. Her restless intellect and constant flow of ideas continually inspire me. Her warmth and generosity of spirit are a welcome and rich part of my life.

My daughter Anja Tranovich, editor extraordinaire, coaxed, cajoled, coached and comforted me throughout the process. I could not have done this without her. It has been one of the great joys and privileges of my life to work with her on this project. My admiration of her goes beyond that of a doting mother as I have come to appreciate her talents in her professional capacity as well as the many personal qualities that make her such a wonderful person and an asset to the planet.

My aunt, Lahoma S Parker, died shortly before publication of this book. She was 97. For the last two years, her keen interest in the book and forceful encouragement has motivated and inspired me. Her love of life and zest for living has been a model for me. As fiercely independent as Queen Melisende herself, she has always been a force to reckon with in our family, and I am ever grateful to have had her in my life.

My husband, Jim Tranovich, tolerated my long absences in the world of the twelfth century and welcomed me back with grace. His loving support sustained me throughout the writing process. My son James is a beacon in my life and a constant source of inspiration. He supported me in this endeavour in his quiet, encouraging way, cheering me with his unique sense of humour. He was always solidly there for me. In their lives and actions, both he and his father serve as a constant reminder to me that a vision and hard work will take you to places you never thought you could go.

In addition to my family, there were so many others. Cheryl Carpenter, whose assistance for the last 26 years has allowed every worthwhile endeavour I have undertaken in that time to come to pass; Julie Ryan, who insisted I follow my heart even when it seemed impossible to do so; supportive friends and colleagues too numerous to mention, lest I leave anyone out; and, of course, the wonderful editorial staff at East & West: Leonard Harrow and Alan Ball.

Margaret Tranovich
California, October 2011

INTRODUCTION

The purpose of this book is to introduce the general reader to the life and times of Queen Melisende. I was first alerted to this fascinating woman by reading about the psalter[1] that bears her name, housed in the British Library. In doing more research on the psalter and its namesake, I wondered why she was not more widely known. Why was there not more information about her? The question I asked has been echoed by almost everyone to whom I have mentioned her name: Queen Melisende? Never heard of her. Who is that?

That is not an easy question to answer. We have no portrait of her. There are no surviving letters or diaries written by her. She is mentioned, mostly in passing, in histories of the Crusades, for she was a Crusader queen. Her reign was right in the middle of the twelfth century, and bridges the time between the establishment of the Crusader kingdoms in 1099, the rule of the first Crusaders, and the loss of Jerusalem to the Muslims in 1187. She wielded power impressively, as will be seen in the recounting of her life experiences.

We have one letter written to her by a leading cleric of the time, Bernard of Clairvaux, and there is a smattering of references to her in historical records. The most illuminating and complete source for information about her is a chronicle written by William, Archbishop of Tyre, usually entitled *A History of Deeds Done Beyond the Sea*. William of Tyre was alive at the end of Queen Melisende's life, and was active in the reign of her younger son, King Amalric, and her grandson, Baldwin IV. Because of his closeness to the royal family, his account may be biased, but it is the most reliable and complete contemporary account we have.

I argue that Queen Melisende's rule comes at a crucial time in the life of the crusading kingdoms. She was a pivotal figure in the continuity of the fragile and fractious Crusader states. As the daughter of a king, the wife of a king, and the mother of a king, she ensured that rulership based on hereditary kingship would prevail and preserve the continuity and cohesion of the kingdom. That there was no objection to her claim to rule speaks volumes in a time when medieval ideas about women served to circumscribe their roles rather than expand them. In fact, that she was able to rule at all tells us something of her character and is a testimony to her spirit and will.

Writing about a woman when so little is known of her personal life, and nothing of her personal feelings, presents many challenges. When we deal with her official life, it is somewhat easier, as that is where the chroniclers focused their reports. Yet even these bear the bias of the writers of the time, and all writers are bound by the ideas and time in which they live.

We have tantalizing clues about the person she must have been: stories of her tenacity in holding on to power; gossip about a sexual liaison; records of her building programmes and artistic patronage. But the story is frustratingly incomplete. In the end we are left with the skeleton of the historical record and our own questions and assumptions of who she might have been.

Sometimes this is a good thing. In works of art, and people from history, it is often what we do not know that keeps us engaged. It is the mystery associated with the subject that keeps us thinking about it. We are free to draw our own conclusions, or not. We can live with the ambiguity, or we can supply our own answers.

Many readers will be unfamiliar with the terrain traversed here. I acknowledge that the twelfth century in general, and the Crusades in particular, may be dimly lit history to most general readers. Most of us have only the barest notion of the Middle Ages. We may, or may not, have a slightly better acquaintance with the Crusades, but without knowing any details. Delving into the twelfth century is bound to be a new experience for most readers. With that in mind, the material is presented in a chronological and narrative fashion. In order to understand the remarkable nature of Queen Melisende's reign, it is necessary to understand the world she inhabited. To that end many pages are spent introducing the reader to life in France in the twelfth century; a brief recounting of the Crusades and the men who embarked on them; an introduction to the Byzantine Empire; and an introduction to the Muslim world in the twelfth century.

While there is no attempt at an in-depth study or analysis of any of these areas, the reader is provided with notes and references that will allow him or her to pursue further knowledge of the subjects.

Though the duration of the Crusades in the Holy Land was about two hundred years, the scope of this book is limited to just the first two-thirds of the twelfth century. The period covered corresponds to the time the Crusaders undertook the First Crusade in 1096, to the time of Queen Melisende's death in 1161. This book is not meant to be a history of the Crusades—there are many other books which cover that topic thoroughly. However, it is not possible to write about Queen Melisende's life without some knowledge of the Crusades, the Crusaders, their struggles and their aims. Some significant events, such as the fiasco of the Second Crusade, are not treated; although it occurred during Queen Melisende's reign, there is no record of her participation in the planning or execution of that ill-fated mission.

After following the progress of the First Crusaders from Constantinople through the lands between there and Jerusalem, the focus is almost exclusively on the kingdom of Jerusalem, and especially the city of Jerusalem, which is where Queen Melisende resided during much of her life, and all of her reign. It was the capital of the kingdom which she ruled, the centre of religious life, and the centre of artistic production, all of which were central to Queen Melisende's life.

I have tried to present a clear picture and stay close to the evidence without over simplifying. This has not been easy. I attempt to indicate the complexity of certain issues without delving into them to the detriment of the narrative or imposing on the patience of the reader.

The story of Queen Melisende is told through the art of her time. The first reason for this is that I am an art historian, and it was the delicacy and beauty of the ivory covers of the book that bears her name that drew me toward the subject. One wonders if we did not have a psalter bearing her name, whether we would know anything about her at all. Secondly, the contributions of Queen Melisende as patron of the arts in her time are irrefutable. It is most often in connection with art that we hear her name mentioned. Certainly in books dealing with Crusader art, she cannot be ignored, for it was her patronage that made possible some of the great architectural and luxury arts of the Crusading period.

Yet consistently, historians and art historians have mentioned her only in passing. She is most often described in histories of the Crusades as being 'married off' to Fulk of Anjou. This was a marriage arranged by her father and the clergy and nobles of the Crusader states. The story generally continues with accounts of Fulk's military campaigns. This is partly because histories of the Crusades tend to focus on the battles and campaigns waged to take and keep the Crusader states. After all, the kingdom was in an almost perpetual state of war. Moreover, the choice of Fulk to be her husband was based on his proven military prowess.

More recent histories have tried to broaden the focus and include more about Queen Melisende, but only occasionally have historians paused to look at the record and give this great Queen her due. One such case was H E Mayer in 1972, in his article, 'Studies in the History of Queen Melisende of Jerusalem', for the *Dumbarton Oaks Papers*. In this paper, he looks closely at the historical records, especially the royal charters, outlining and filling in our knowledge of the Queen and her activities.

Yet in spite of his meticulous and detailed report, her role as monarch and patron of the arts is known to but a small group of scholars, and only a handful of them have written in any detail about her and her reign. To the latter this book is deeply indebted, and I have drawn liberally from their work. Yet the question remains why, almost forty years after Mayer's study, this is the first full-length non-fiction book to deal with Queen Melisende's life and legacy?

Certainly part of the reason is that she was a woman. History in general has treated women lightly, both because of bias and because history reflects the power structure and tends to be written by, for and about men. The treatment of women in historical context tends to be determined by the prevailing mores and attitudes about gender at the time the history was written. This book does not purport to be any different in this regard.

Since the time of her rule there have been a multitude of books about the Crusades, nearly all of them, especially before the last ten years or so, written by men. Thus certain ideas get passed on and solidified from generation to generation, as authors read and quote other authors. When one remembers that the books, ideas, academic milieu and publishing world were all dominated by men until recently, it is no wonder that our Queen has been hidden and forgotten. Perhaps the chronicles of the time especially reflect this. The twelfth century, dominated in Europe as it was by the Church and its negative attitude toward women, gave very little credence to anything feminine, especially women who were, or wanted to be, powerful. Chroniclers of the Crusades were products of this cultural bias. Thus it is not surprising that they rarely mention Queen Melisende. We might think it remarkable that William of Tyre has anything good to say about her. That at times he fairly gushes his admiration is in itself a testimony to the strength of her character.

As difficult as it was for historians to include Queen Melisende's accomplishments in histories written since her time due to the attitudes of Church and society towards women, current authors find less difficulty approaching her reign with a more open mind, and perhaps a more generous reading of the historical record. Certainly histories of the Crusades written in the last ten years give Queen Melisende more credit and print-space than ever before. This is not because the historical sources have changed, indeed they have not. It is that these sources are open to interpretation, and even the language used in quoting them can change their impact from author to author. For example, to describe a queen as 'power hungry', but a king as 'in control', indicates the bias of the author which influences the reader as well.

Nevertheless, it is not always necessary to cloak discussions of power in gender. In Queen Melisende's case, the nobles who were in power at the time of her accession apparently did not see her as a threat, but for what she was: the best hope for the survival and continuity of the fragile Crusader states. Her apparent skill at diplomacy and expertise and experience with administrating and managing the affairs of the kingdom made her an extremely effective, if forgotten, ruler.

I will admit that she utterly captivated me, and I hope something of my fascination with her comes through to the reader. In this book I have tried to present an informed picture of her life. By presenting what we do know about her, we can at least bring her out from the shadows of history and shine a light on her accomplishments. We can put her in the context of her time and place. We can reclaim her for ourselves and posterity.

These ideas were brought home to me by the granddaughter of a friend who asked me what I was writing. When I told her about this forgotten queen, her eyes lit up, and I saw in them the recognition that she was the inheritor of this story. Here was a flesh and blood antidote to the fairy-tale princesses of her reading experience; a real, true historical figure who lived and loved and wielded power and ruled a kingdom on her own. This is the power of women's history— recognition that we are part of a legacy, even if it has been hidden and forgotten. It is all the more significant for that.

The first chapter introduces us to Queen Melisende and some of the significant events of her life. We will look in some detail at the front cover of the Queen Melisende Psalter, and see what the images carved there in ivory tell us about the expectations of rulers in the twelfth century. It is there that we discover clues to the story behind the commission of the psalter. We will read what others had to say about her. As we examine some of the challenges she faced in her reign, we can get a sense of her personality in how she dealt with them.

In the following chapter, life in Europe and the circumstances surrounding the First Crusade are examined. This will tell us something about the Europe from which Queen Melisende's father and the other Crusaders came. It must be remembered that Europe was not a cohesive political unit in the twelfth century with the familiar modern national entities of today. There was fragmentation within these regions and the boundaries dividing them were constantly shifting. We will explore the underlying causes and motivation for the First Crusade and gain a good picture of the world the Crusaders lived in and left. That will allow us to appreciate the contrast of that world with those they encountered in Byzantium and the Islamic Empire. Those who embarked on the First Crusade would leave the life they had known behind, some forever, all for at least five years. In many ways the journey they were taking would change them and the world they left in ways unimaginable when the Crusades began.

Chapter 3 will introduce us to the rich and powerful Byzantine Empire. This empire was already many centuries old by the time the Crusaders arrived there. In contrast to the Europe from which the Crusaders came, its governmental structures and court rituals were highly developed and well-established. As the most dominant power in the region, it was the Byzantine court against which all other courts and powers measured themselves. This competition spanned all areas, from political intrigue to production of luxury objects. It was this empire, more than Europe, which was threatened by the incursion of Muslim forces. The Byzantines and Muslims had been fighting over territory for centuries, but there was a new Muslim force in the region, the Seljuk Turks, and the balance of power was beginning to shift in their favour, much to the alarm and consternation of the Byzantines. At the same time, the Byzantine attitudes towards those forces differed significantly from that of the Crusaders. This was to present difficulties in the relationship between the two groups from the outset.

Westerners had little exposure and less understanding of the Islamic empire they encountered as they continued on their journey to the Holy Land. Luckily for the Crusaders, the Islamic world was involved in so much internal turmoil within its ranks that it did not fully grasp the significance of the invasion that would so challenge and change the shape of its world. As the two cultures came into closer contact, however, Westerners developed a certain grudging admiration and acceptance of the clothing, customs, food, and art of the Muslims. After examining these aspects of their culture in Chapter 4, we will understand why.

We arrive in Chapter 5 at the court of Queen Melisende herself. Here we will examine the extent of her artistic patronage in and around Jerusalem. Her life and works reflected the richness and refinement of the Byzantine and Islamic cultures alongside certain customs and ideas of the West. Because of its unique position geographically, politically and culturally, the court of Queen Melisende was at the centre of contact of three great artistic and cultural traditions: European, Byzantine, and Islamic. We will see how the art produced during her reign reflects this reality.

In Chapter 6 we focus on how the mingling of artistic traditions that took place during Queen Melisende's reign flowed from there into Europe. The revival of Western art is usually attributed to the sack of Constantinople in 1204 by the members of the Fourth Crusade. The religious and secular treasures of that city were taken back to Europe and found their way to every corner of it. It cannot be denied that this flood of objects had a huge impact on artistic production there. However, prior to that, art objects from the court of Queen Melisende made their way back to Europe. Religious mementos like pieces of the True Cross (the cross upon which Christ was believed to have been crucified) were especially treasured, and housed in the most magnificent containers decorated with gold and precious gems. These objects introduced Western artists to designs and motifs that were not common in Europe. They differed from Byzantine art in that they reflected a combination of styles including Byzantine, Islamic and Western. We will see how they were absorbed and integrated by Western culture, and continued to influence it for years to come.

My journey to discover and uncover the story of Queen Melisende has been both fascinating and enlightening. I continue to marvel at her skill in establishing and holding onto power in an age when the attitudes toward women did not make room for either. I admire her strength of character and self-confidence. Her life had all the things that books and movies are made of: a powerful figure, scandal, intrigue, tragedy. All the more amazing is that this is not a current figure, but a woman who lived and prospered nine hundred years ago.

It would make a great fairy tale—except it is true. In deference to my six-year-old friend mentioned earlier, let us start our journey in this way: Once upon a time, in a kingdom long ago and far away, there lived a rich and powerful queen …

1
FORGOTTEN QUEEN

In a display case in the museum of the British Library are the carved ivory book covers of the Queen Melisende Psalter. In the low-lit interior of the case, it is difficult, but just possible, to discern aspects of the dense rich carving. There are roundels with scenes, and figures between and around the medallions (col. pls 1.1 and 1.2). There is a border filled with highly decorative foliate designs interspersed with urns and animals, and in places, interlace design. It is all very crowded, and there is hardly a space where some action is not taking place.

Originally the entire cover was gilded, the gold leaf creating an effect similar to the exquisite gold work of the time. The profusion of images and decoration create an impact that is reminiscent of the *horror vacuii* ('the fear of empty space') often ascribed to Islamic decoration. But in the six roundels, we see a programme that is decidedly Western. It is here that we see scenes from the life of King David from the Old Testament. Each medallion is meticulously carved, with identifying inscriptions and careful composition. This level of detail, carved in ivory, in the space of only 21.6 by 14 cm. is astounding. These scenes encapsulate the role of kingship as understood by medieval rulers.

What does it all mean? What are these pictures about? Who is Queen Melisende? Why is this psalter named after her? Is this just a beautiful work of art, or does it have a story? Does it tell us anything about the woman after whom it is named?

These are good questions for any art historian, or curious onlooker, to ask. And for this work, like any great work of art, the answers to these questions lead us on a journey of discovery; a journey into a time and place long ago and far away; into a world few of us know

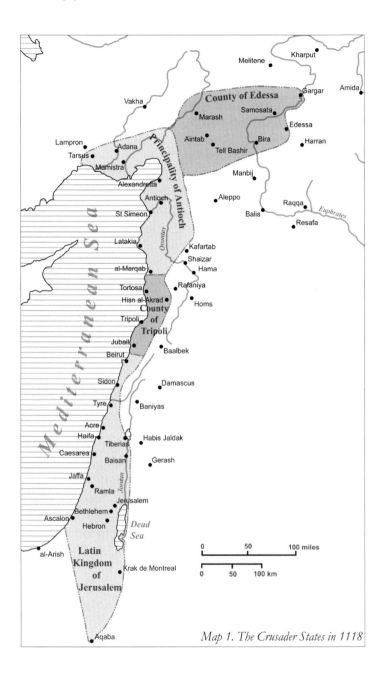

Map 1. The Crusader States in 1118

much about; into the world of hidden power and a forgotten queen. The setting is the kingdom established by the first Crusaders in 1099.

It is 1131 and the king of Jerusalem is dying. We can imagine his thoughts. It is a critical moment in the life of the fledgling kingdom of Jerusalem. From the time when he fought alongside his cousin, King Baldwin I, the first king of Jerusalem, King Baldwin II had been fighting dissension within the crusader kingdom itself, as the nobles from the First Crusade struggled among themselves for power and property. This and the constant threat of the Muslims menacing the borders had required much of his time and energy.

Of his four daughters, it is Melisende, the firstborn, whom he has come to trust with the administration of the kingdom while he was on the battlefield. He has trained her from an early age in the affairs of the kingdom. He had her sign documents, with her name alongside his, so that her authority would be respected.[1] He chose her husband carefully. Out of the many candidates to be her husband, he needed a powerful and courageous man who was an experienced fighter, for the one thing his daughter could not do was fight.

Marriages in the Middle Ages were not love matches. They were political, social and economic alliances. King Baldwin II's own marriage had been with the aim of establishing a strong bond between the Armenian community of Edessa and the Crusaders from France. His wife, Morphia, was an Armenian princess. She brought with her not only the political advantage of alliance with her powerful father, but also a rich dowry which helped to finance the continuation of the kingdom.[2]

Edessa was one of the first cities to be conquered in the First Crusade. The city itself was ruled by Armenian Christians. It lay between the encroaching Muslim Seljuk Turks and the Byzantine Empire. It had been under Byzantine rule, but was anxious to throw off the yoke of the Byzantine Empire, with its high taxes and insistence on orthodoxy. The Crusaders were welcomed and embraced as liberators.[3]

From the Crusaders' point of view, Edessa and the surrounding areas provided a buffer between the Muslims and the Crusader territories to the south and west. Because of its rich agricultural lands, it also provided a valuable supply route and resources to provision the Crusaders advancing through Anatolia. In this way, the left flank of the main Crusading army could be fortified and protected.[4]

The first Crusader ruler of Edessa was Baldwin II's cousin, Baldwin I. Baldwin I was brother to the first Crusader ruler of Jerusalem, Godfrey. When Godfrey died in 1100, Baldwin I was summoned to Jerusalem to succeed his brother as king. He invested his cousin, Baldwin II, with Edessa and the surrounding territories, making him the second Count of Edessa. It was at this point that Baldwin II married Morphia, daughter of Gabriel, lord of Melitene.[5] By this act he consolidated his position in the area, gained powerful allies within the Armenian community, and obtained financial backing from his wealthy Armenian father-in-law.

When Baldwin I died in 1118, Baldwin II, in his turn, became King of Jerusalem. He was one of the last survivors of the original group of knights of the First Crusade. Baldwin II had been tested in battle and was trusted and welcomed by the council of clergy and nobles in Jerusalem. He was unanimously elected king by this Council.[6] This act established continuity of rule in the Latin Kingdoms at a critical time.

King Baldwin II and his wife, Morphia, had four daughters. Melisende was the eldest. Recognizing that he had no male heir to succeed him, King Baldwin had involved Melisende in affairs of the kingdom.[7] The issue of a suitable husband for her must have been a subject of much discussion and considerable concern.

The king consulted his council in Jerusalem, and also sent an envoy to the King of France, Louis VI, to get his advice about an appropriate candidate for marriage to his daughter. Louis VI recommended Fulk, Count of Anjou. This recommendation was supported by Pope Honorius II.[8] Fulk was forty years old and a widower. Chronicler William of Tyre describes him:

(He was) a ruddy man, like David, whom the Lord found
after His own heart. He was faithful and gentle, affable,
kind, and compassionate, unusual traits in people of that
complexion. In works of piety and the giving of alms, he
was most generous. Even before he was called to guide
the affairs of the kingdom, he was a powerful prince
… He was an experienced warrior full of patience and
wisdom in military affairs. He was of medium height
and was already well advanced in age.[9]

Fulk had been on a pilgrimage to Jerusalem in 1120 and had
met King Baldwin II. In addition, he had the other prime requisite
to be a future King of Jerusalem—he was an experienced fighting
man. Fulk had relinquished his lands in France in favour of his
son, Geoffrey (recently married to the Empress Matilda, heir to the
throne of England and Normandy).[10] The prospect of marriage to
the young Melisende was secondary to the opportunity to become
King of Jerusalem. His agreement with Baldwin II was based upon
this certainty.[11] They married in May, 1129.

The Crusader states faced a chronic shortage of fighting men, and
controlled only pockets of territory. When Fulk came from his territories
in France, he brought much needed trained and equipped fighting men
with him. They were loyal to Fulk, Baldwin knew. He also knew they
would expect to be rewarded for their loyalty. But it was crucial that the
kingdom be held together, not just by being united in fighting the infidel,
but by a dynasty of rulers that could continue from one generation to
the next. Already Melisende and Fulk had given him a grandson, his
namesake, Baldwin III, a boy who would also grow up to be King of
Jerusalem. He must make sure of that. He would not leave an opening
for Fulk to abandon his daughter and marry someone else, as had
happened already in the short history of the Crusader states.

On his deathbed, King Baldwin II called his daughter, Melisende,
her husband Fulk of Anjou, and their two-year-old son Baldwin III
to his bedside and summoned the closest nobles and churchmen to

witness his next act. There, 'in the presence of the lord Patriarch and the prelates and such nobles as happened to be there', he transferred power to Melisende, Fulk, and Baldwin jointly.[12] He did this to make clear to the family and the nobles of the kingdom that he meant Fulk to rule as joint sovereign with Melisende and their son. This would ensure both the continuity of Queen Melisende's involvement in the management of the kingdom, and the continuity of his bloodline as ruler, no matter what happened to Fulk.

Ibn al-Qalanisi (1073-1160), a Muslim historian, writes of King Baldwin II's death:

> In this year (526/1131-32) news came from the Franks of the death of Baldwin, 'the little leader' (al-ru'ays), King of the Franks and Lord of Jerusalem. He died in Acre on Thursday 25 Ramadan/8 August 1132 (this date is not correct: Baldwin died at Jerusalem on 21 August, 1131 which corresponds to 25 Ramadan 525). He was an old man, rich in experience and inured to every trial and hardship of life. Several times he had been imprisoned by the Muslims, in war and in peace, but his famous stratagems and skilful manoeuvring had got him out. At his death he was succeeded by a man who lacked his good sense and fit for kingship; the King was Fulk, Count of Anjou, who came out by sea from his homeland. Baldwin's death caused trouble and disturbance among the Franks.[13]

Baldwin II was buried in the Church of the Holy Sepulchre next to Godfrey and Baldwin I, the previous rulers of Jerusalem.[14] When the king died, there erupted a power struggle between Queen Melisende, aligned with the (mostly Norman) nobles of the kingdom, and King Fulk.[15]

Rarely have husband and wife quarrelled with so much at stake. This disturbance alluded to by Ibn al-Qalanasi involved a revolt by the resident nobility, led by Count Hugh of Jaffa, and was a reaction to Fulk's attempt to replace old magnates with new ones who were mostly from Anjou.

Orderic Vitalis, a writer living at the time, wrote these words about King Fulk which explain the dispute:

> To begin with he acted without the foresight and shrewdness he should have shown, and changed governors and other dignitaries too quickly and thoughtlessly. As a new ruler he banished from his counsels the leading magnates who from the first had fought resolutely against the Turks and helped Godfrey and the two Baldwins to bring towns and fortresses under their rule, and replaced them with Angevin strangers and other raw newcomers to whom he gave his ear; turning out the veteran defenders, he gave the chief places in the counsels of the realm and the proprietorship of castles to new flatterers. Consequently great disaffection spread, and the stubbornness of the magnates was damnably roused against the man who changed officials so gauchely.[16]

In addition, there were rumours of an affair between the Queen and Count Hugh, of whom William of Tyre said:

> In him the gifts of nature seemed to have met in lavish abundance; without question, in respect to physical beauty and nobility of birth, as well as experience in the art of war, he had no equal in the kingdom.'[17]

Hugh was accused of treason, which he denied. In the end, Hugh was sentenced to be exiled for three years. Before he could leave for his exile, he was attacked in Jerusalem. King Fulk was suspected to be behind the attack, however the attacker admitted to acting alone.

Count Hugh did finally leave for his exile. He died in Sicily before he could return to his home in the Holy Land.[18]

The result of this whole situation was an escalation of hostility whereby Fulk and his allies were not safe at court when the queen and her allies were present. Queen Melisende, far from being submissive, was willing to take on her husband and his followers in order to preserve the existing power structure. In this she was supported by the other nobles. Surely these actions alone would have been enough to establish the stature and resolve of this young queen. That the other nobles respected her enough to support her shows that they took her seriously, whether or not in spite of the fact that she was a woman, we do not know. That her husband and his followers were afraid of her is likewise an indication of the power she fearlessly wielded. The rumours about her relationship with Count Hugh of Jaffa, which could have been fabricated by her husband and his countrymen, were, and still are, typically used as a way of discrediting and undermining female assertions of power by tarnishing their reputations and turning the tide of public opinion against them. That this story was widely reported and remarked upon, both at the time, and by later historians, shows the age-old fascination with scandal involving those in high places. We also cannot discount the possibility, even probability, of the stories being a response to Queen Melisende's power and almost an obligation in reflecting the prevailing view of women during the period.

Scholars have given other reasons for these rumours: that Fulk was looking for an excuse to discredit and discard Melisende,[19] that the rumours were to divert the public from the unpopularity of Fulk's rule,[20] or to mask the fact that Fulk was trying to push the queen aside and rule independently from her.[21]

Whatever the reason, the strategy did not work, and the situation was eventually resolved through the intervention of third parties, with considerable concessions on both sides. After this incident, they shared in the governing of the kingdom. It is said that, from 1136 forward, King Fulk did not act in matters large or small without the consent of Queen Melisende.[22] Her participation in the rule of the kingdom is demonstrated by the fact that her name appears, along with Fulk's, on the royal charters issued after their reconciliation.[23]

The Queen Melisende Psalter, with the rich imagery of its ivory covers and the superior quality of its contents, is thought to be a gift symbolizing this reconciliation.

Each of the main scenes on the front (col. pls 1.1, 1.2) are emphasized by the use of a curving, swirling scrollwork that encapsulates the stories and separates them from the smaller figures and vignettes that surround them. The scenes represented are from the life of King David. As the most famous Old Testament ruler, and precursor of Christ, King David was considered an ancestor and model for medieval rulers. In illustrating the heroic and inspirational acts of King David's reign, Fulk, who likely commissioned this book, would be making reference to his own qualities of strength and valour, thereby reflecting his own ability to rule. If we look closely and think deeply about each scene, we can see what virtues of kingship were valued in the Middle Ages. The first scene shows David protecting his lamb from the lion and the bear (1 Samuel 17, 34-36). The medieval ruler was expected to protect his 'flock', his subjects, from outside dangers, just as the Crusaders were perceived to be protecting the Holy Land from the Muslims.

Next to it is the scene of David being anointed by Samuel in front of a building inscribed 'Bethleheem' while God's hand blesses him from above (I Samuel 16, 13). This is an obvious reference to God's blessing of the taking of Jerusalem from the 'infidels' by the Crusaders. This reference would not include Fulk, as he was not one of the original Crusaders, but it would include Queen Melisende, by reference to her father who participated in the battle to liberate Jerusalem.

Below the first medallion is the story of David and Goliath. It is the quintessential story of right over might, of the underdog winning against all odds. This would be an apt description of the role of the Crusaders who overcame so many hardships to take Jerusalem. It also affirms the Crusaders' belief that it was their right and duty, as Christians, to liberate Jerusalem and other Christian sites from the infidel.

Next to it is the story of David, who fled from Saul and was received by Ahimelech ('Abimelec' as inscribed here) who was a priest in the city of Nob. He has the spear of Goliath and the holy bread of the altar. This could also refer to the Crusaders, the city of Jerusalem, and the holy relics preserved there.

The lower left medallion is discussed below and the last scene is of King David at peace, playing his harp and surrounded by musicians. A dove, representing the Holy Spirit, but also perhaps the dove of peace, is whispering into his ear. Music and peace, and all is right with the world after the struggle portrayed in the other scenes.

Between the medallions are representations of the Virtues and Vices in combat. These images are taken from a fifth-century poem by Aurelius Prudentius Clemens and reinforce the ideas depicted in the medallions.[24] They are used to make an additional point about the role of kings: that the king (Virtue) does battle with the evils besetting the kingdom (Vices) in order to protect and defend the people in his charge. Thus the king defends the moral virtue of the kingdom. This symbolism was particularly rich and meaningful to the Crusaders, who had risked and sometimes lost their lives in order to rid the holy places of Christendom of the infidel. The need to preserve peace by using violence is the background for the scenes of David, who is for the most part (except for the slaying of Goliath) involved in protective or penitential acts.

It is in the scene of the lower left roundel that scholars believe holds the secret to the origin of this remarkable book.[25] Meticulously carved in a space less than two inches in diameter, we see King David kneeling before an altar with a flame on it. Above the king's head is a banner inscribed *ego peccavi* ('I have sinned'). He is kneeling before the prophet Gad, who is holding a scroll inscribed *construe altare D(omi) no* ('construct an altar to God'). This scene describes the repentance of King David for ordering the census of his people (II Samuel, 24, 10-25). Because his pride had incited him to number those in his kingdom, David was punished by the Lord who sent a plague against his people. David asks to be punished himself, rather than have the people suffer, and so the Lord orders him to construct an altar. This altar is to be on the site of the future Temple of Jerusalem. Behind David is the crenellated wall where we see God's hand coming out of a cloud to hold back an angel holding a spear of retribution.

Looking further at the context of the roundel within the scheme of decoration, we see two pairs of the personification of Virtues and Vices battling each other. To the left are Sobrietas and Luxuria, and to the right Fortitudo and Avaritia. The two vices pictured, Luxuria (luxury) and Aviritia (greed), are considered to be the two primary temptations of the secular world and are connected to King David (and thus medieval kings as well) through his lust for Bathsheba and his greed in ordering the census. His genuine repentance and building of the altar show the qualities of Fortitudo (fortitude) and Sobrietas (sobriety, restraint).[26]

We can read the scene as paralleling the real life situation of Queen Melisende and King Fulk. King Fulk repents of his pride in presuming to take over the kingdom from Queen Melisende and the 'old guard' nobility loyal to her; she recognizes his sacrifices on behalf of the kingdom and King Baldwin II. Together they undertake to rebuild the Temple as a sign of true repentance and a covenant with God.[27] The 'Temple' is the Church of the Holy Sepulchre, the site of the tomb of Christ. It was the holiest Christian monument in Jerusalem and invested with reverence and sentiment by every Crusader and pilgrim.

The battle between the Virtues and Vices, just above and between the last two roundels, contributes to this reading: struggle (the battle) and perseverance (fortitude) are necessary to overcome enemies within and without, and lead to moral victory (sobriety over luxury). The final roundel embodies this sentiment as King David plays his harp (the source of solace and peace for Saul) along with other musicians. There is once again harmony in the home and in the kingdom.

We can only imagine Queen Melisende's reaction when she held the psalter in her hands for the first time. It must have been with feelings of awe and pleasure, not unlike the reaction of a viewer today. The intricately carved ivory covers were covered in gold in order to give the impression that they were made of that precious metal. On such a gilded and reflective surface, the turquoise, rubies and carbuncles that were distributed on its surface would have shown even more than they do today.

Was it this initial reaction she would remember instead of their five-year feud, when, several years later, she saw the dead body of her husband?

King Fulk fought valiantly in defence of the kingdom. The story of his exploits is widely and thoroughly documented in historical annals. He died, not on the battlefield fighting the infidel, but in a hunting accident. William of Tyre, chronicler of Queen Melisende's reign, gives us this detailed account:

> It happened in those days, when autumn was over, that the king and queen were sojourning for a time at the city of Acre. In order to vary the monotony by some agreeable recreations, the queen expressed a desire to go out of the city to a certain place in the suburbs where there were many springs. That she might not lack the pleasure of his company, the king attended her with his usual escort. As they were riding along, the servants who had preceded the train happened to rouse a hare which was lying in a furrow. It fled, followed by the shouts of all. The king, impelled by evil fate, seized his lance and joined the pursuit. In vigorous chase, he began to urge on his horse in that direction. Finally, the steed, driven to reckless speed, stumbled and fell. The king was thrown headforemost to the ground. As he lay there stunned by the pain of the fall, the saddle struck his head and his brains gushed forth from both ears and nostrils. The members of his escort,

those in advance and those following him, overcome with horror at the frightful accident, rushed to his aid as he lay on the ground. They found him unconscious, however, unable to speak or understand.

When the queen was informed of her husband's unexpected death, she was pierced to the heart by the sinister disaster: She tore her garments and hair and by her loud shrieks and lamentations gave proof of her intense grief. Flinging herself upon the ground she embraced the lifeless body. Tears failed her through continual weeping; frequent sobs interrupted her voice, as she tried to give expression to her grief …

The king's deplorable accident soon became known. Rumour, on swift wings, spread the news throughout the city of Acre. Crowds flocked to the scene, all eager to convince themselves of the unspeakable disaster. Tearfully they bore him thence to the city, where he lived until the third day, unconscious but still breathing. Thus, on November 10, in the year 1142 of the incarnation of our Lord and of Fulk's reign the eleventh, his life was brought to a close in a good old age. [He was 53.][28]

Fulk was buried, like his father-in-law and the other Crusader rulers, in the Church of the Holy Sepulchre.[29]

In spite of the tragedy of her husband's death, Queen Melisende rose to the challenges now presented to her. Her two young sons were still too young to rule. The elder, called Baldwin after his maternal grandfather, was thirteen. The younger, Amalric, was six. We can assume that when her husband was away fighting battles, both with the Muslims and his own vassals, Queen Melisende was in charge of managing the kingdom. It seems to have been quite acceptable to the council and the nobles residing in Jerusalem that the queen would rule as regent for her son, for we have no record of any dissent to this act. Accordingly, Queen Melisende and Baldwin III were 'anointed, consecrated, and crowned' together in the Church of the Holy Sepulchre. The ceremony was conducted by William, patriarch of Jerusalem, in the presence of the 'princes and all the prelates of the church'.[30]

We can only imagine the challenges of a woman ruling a kingdom in the twelfth century. Unable to lead an army into battle, she had to depend on loyal nobles and, eventually, her son to ensure security of the kingdom and its borders. She could advise and strategize, but not fight.

In many ways, she had to navigate the treacherous waters of the expectations of her as a woman, and the expectations of her as a ruler. These two positions were often at odds. An illustration of that is the advice she received from one of the great clerics of the time, Bernard of Clairvaux:

> You must set your hand to great things and, although a woman, you must act as a man by doing all you have to do 'in a spirit prudent and strong'. You must arrange all things prudently and discreetly, so that all may judge you from your actions to be a king rather than a queen and so that the Gentiles may have no occasion for saying: Where is the king of Jerusalem? But you will say: Such things are beyond my power; they are great matters of a man and I am only a woman, weak in body, changeable of heart, not far-seeing in counsel nor accustomed to business.[31]

It is tempting to say that in fact, from what we know of Queen Melisende, she would have said none of those things, for she was raised to rule by her father, and ruled capably in the absence of her husband. She was, from what we can tell from the affairs of the kingdom, very much accustomed to business and politically shrewd. This might not have been clear, or even conceivable to Bernard of Clairvaux, but it must have been obvious to the nobles and citizens of the Latin Kingdom, for she was unanimously approved by the council to become queen and regent for her son.

William of Tyre had this to say about Queen Melisende at the time:

> Melisende, the king's mother, was a woman of great wisdom who had had much experience in all kinds of secular matters. She had risen so far above the normal status of women that she dared to undertake important measures. It was her ambition to emulate the magnificence of the greatest and noblest princes and to show herself in no wise inferior to them. Since her son was as yet under age, she ruled the kingdom and administered the government with such skilful care that she may be said truly to have equalled her ancestors in that respect.[32]

During this period she continued her patronage of ecclesiastic building. This included the remodelling of the Church of the Holy Sepulchre begun by her and Fulk. The newly remodelled church was dedicated in 1149. A true daughter of the region, she was both comfortable with and used to the highest quality of luxury goods available in the area. These would have included objects produced in both Muslim lands and the Byzantine Empire. Like many of the children of Westerners who had come with the first Crusaders, she was fully acculturated and immersed in an Eastern culture and way of life.

As queen, she was the link between the generation of the First Crusaders, which included her father, and the children and heirs of that group who struggled to hold on to the kingdom in the face of continuing assault both from within and without. As daughter of a king, wife of a king, and mother of a king, she provided continuity and stability in a kingdom badly in need of both.

She continued to rule long after Baldwin III reached the age of majority at fifteen. He was twenty-two when he demanded to be crowned as an adult ruler. The queen wanted to be crowned jointly with him to ensure their shared responsibility for the kingdom. But Baldwin III arranged secretly to be crowned alone, and there began a rift between mother and son that split the kingdom. They each had their supporters and a compromise was reached. Queen Melisende would retain control of Jerusalem, Nablus, and the coast where Amalric, the younger son, held the County of Jaffa. Baldwin III would control Galilee and the north.[33]

At a time when the Muslim armies were waiting for any opening, such a partition of the kingdom was untenable. Baldwin III gradually asserted his claim to the whole of the kingdom. Queen Melisende kept Nablus.[34]

About the rift with her son, Baldwin III, William of Tyre remarks:

> As long as her son was willing to be governed by her counsel, the people enjoyed a highly desirable state of tranquillity, and the affairs of the realm moved on prosperously. But the more frivolous elements in the kingdom soon found that the queen's wise influence hindered their attempts to draw the king into their own pursuits. They therefore persuaded their royal master, who like others of his age, was 'pliable as wax in being bent toward vice, but rough toward those who rebuked him,' to withdraw from the guardianship of his mother and to rule the kingdom of his fathers himself ... Although this intrigue originated in the thoughtless levity or malice of certain individuals, it came near being the ruin of the whole kingdom.[35]

Even after the resolution of the conflict with her son, Queen Melisende continued to be involved in affairs of the kingdom, albeit to a much smaller degree. Her name appears in royal charters up to 1157. At some point after this, according to William of Tyre, she fell ill 'of an incurable disease for which there was no help except death.'[36]

We have this reference from William of Tyre on the occasion of her death in 1161:

> Transcending the strength of women, the lady queen, Melisende, a prudent woman, discreet above the female sex, had ruled the kingdom with fitting moderation for more than thirty years, during the lifetime of her husband and the reign of her son.[37]

Queen Melisende was buried in Jerusalem at the Tomb of the Virgin in the valley of Jehoshaphat. Her mother, Morphia, had been buried there in the late 1120s. The tradition of burying queens near the tomb of the Virgin Mary, and kings near the tomb of Christ in the Church of the Holy Sepulchre was already established at the time of her death.[38]

If she looked at her psalter again after her husband's death, or at the time of her coronation with her son, would the symbolism of the front covers have been even more meaningful? Would she have looked at those scenes from the life of David and felt the weight of her responsibility all the more? Would she have looked again at the back cover, with the scenes of the acts of mercy, and re-evaluated her role and goals for the kingdom? After her difficulties with her son, would she have turned to the psalter once more and looked in the pages of the book for solace in the prayers found there? Would she once again marvel at its beauty as she reflected on her life?

Though we can never know the answers to these questions, this book and the life of Queen Melisende are intertwined in the most profound and uncanny way. In much the same way as the scenes on the covers are connected by their spiralling borders, the significant events in Queen Melisende's life evolve and unfold, tied together by fate and the responsibilities devolved on her by the people and events in her life: her father as he prepared her to rule the kingdom; her husband as he vied with her for power; Fulk's death and her rule as queen in her own right; her son's challenge to her power.

The book reminds us of the characteristics of kingship as seen by the twelfth-century mind. It shows us the role of leadership and stewardship that was expected of rulers. That Queen Melisende abided by these tenets, and lived up to them, as a woman who ruled in her own right over a fractious kingdom, gives us the opportunity to appreciate and marvel at her abilities and contributions anew.

If we accept that art reflects the time and culture in which it is made, we can expect that close examination of the covers and content of the Queen Melisende Psalter will reveal something to us about its namesake. We will especially look closely at the circumstances surrounding the making of it. But first we must understand more about the world that Queen Melisende inhabited. We must understand where she came from, the influences that shaped her, the circumstances that formed her personality. To understand all of that, we will need to take the journey her father took; follow in the footsteps of the First Crusaders; become acquainted with the world Queen Melisende inhabited, and follow the development of her life.

2
THE CRUSADES

It must have been an astonishing experience for those first Crusaders. Most of them had only rarely been out of the confines of their own region, much less their own country. They could not have had even the dimmest idea of what was awaiting them. For many, it would be death, sweetened by the assurance of the pope that their souls would go straight to heaven as a reward for giving their life to fight the infidel, and rid the most Holy City of Christendom of the heathens. For others who would survive to reach the Holy City, it would be the satisfaction of reaching their goal and accomplishing their objective, and the joy of returning home to tell about it. For still others, a relatively small group, it would be life in a foreign land, and property and power which had been denied them in the country of their origin. This group would spend the rest of their lifetimes fighting to hold on to what they had won.

The most common description of life in Europe during the Middle Ages is that there were three classes of people: those who fight, those who pray, and those who work. The first two classes, the nobles and the clergy, comprised only five to ten percent of the total population. The craftsmen, merchants, artisans and peasants who made up the working class accounted for ninety to ninety-five percent of the population.

There was no notion or possibility of upward mobility between the classes in the twelfth century. Each group had their place and was expected to do the best job they could in the role assigned to them.

While we tend to think of the classes being separate, their lives were inextricably entwined. In the feudal system that existed, simply

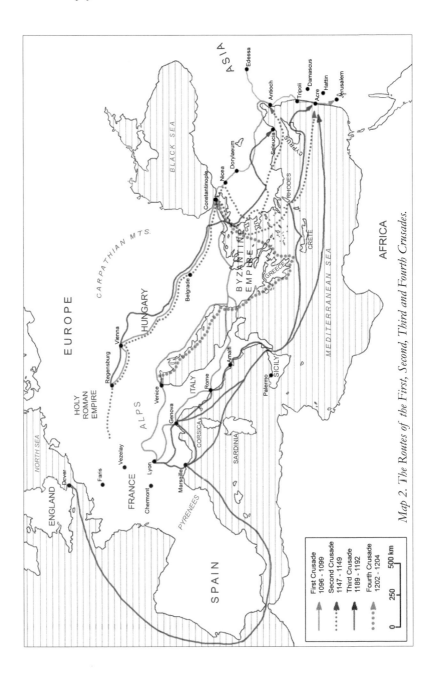

Map 2. The Routes of the First, Second, Third and Fourth Crusades.

stated, the noble gave the peasant land of his own to farm in exchange for the labour of the peasant on the lord's land and protection in time of conflict. While the peasant would not have personal contact with the noble on a daily basis, the relationship was dictated by the roles each played in the life of the other.

The relationship between the Church and the nobles was somewhat more complex. Until the Protestant Reformation of the sixteenth century, there was only one Church in Europe, headed by the pope in Rome. Many of the high-ranking clergy of the great bureaucracy associated with the Church were drawn from the noble class. It was a time when religion and society were closely intertwined, and there was never a clear division between Church and state. The two were often in conflict over power and status.[1] Pope Urban II, who called for the First Crusade and about whom we will talk later, was from a noble family in the Champagne region of northern France. One scholar asserts that it is this combination of noble blood and religious calling that gave the pope the skills to call for Crusade and have the call appeal to so many.[2]

Agriculture was the primary occupation of the majority of the people and the greatest source of wealth for the few who owned the land in the period. Northern Europe in the eleventh and twelfth centuries was benefiting from increased prosperity that came from improvements and innovations in agriculture of the previous centuries. Watermills, deep and efficient ploughs, the three-year cycle of crops (wheat, then oats or barley, then fallow), and the cultivation of virgin land allowed for an abundance that both created and supported the expanding population. Many of the members of that increased population moved into the cities. As urban populations grew, demand for goods and specialization of labour also grew.

But it was still agriculture that dominated the lives of the vast majority of the population. Understanding daily life in the twelfth century will give us insight into both the world the Crusaders left, and also how they may have reacted to life in the lands they were about to encounter.

For peasant and lord alike, the interrelationship of the seasons of the year, the agricultural tasks performed, and the religious festivals created a rhythm and regularity to life. The tasks of agricultural workers were illustrated in sculptural decoration on the outside of churches, wooden carving of choir seats in the interior of churches, and illuminated manuscripts. These served to confirm and celebrate the dominance and importance of agriculture in the lives of the entire medieval population. In the illustration from a twelfth-century English illuminated manuscript (col. plate 2.1), we see the labours of four months coupled with the astrological sign ruling that month. Note how the feet of the labourers extend beyond the roundels reserved for them, as if the exuberance and creativity of the artist cannot be contained in such a small space. The symbols for the astrological signs also show the spirit of the artists and reflect the interest of the medieval viewer in strange and mythical beasts.

In the month of September, the astrological sign Libra is shown next to an image of a labourer working amidst grape vines, as this was the time of the grape harvest. In the next scene on the same page, the sign for Scorpio (in an inventive and whimsical image) a worker is shown sowing seeds, the labour for that month. Below, the bow-wielding centaur as Sagittarius is shown connected to an image of an axe-wielding man killing a pig, announcing the season of butchering meat. This labour of November provided some meat for the winter. Every part of the animal would be used, including the ears, tail and snout and all of the internal organs. In further preparation for winter, the labourer in the next image collects wood. The sea-goat symbolizing the astrological sign of Capricorn is the sign for December. This strange creature has the upper body and head of a goat, and the lower body of a sea creature and is imaginatively depicted by the artist.

The way the astrological signs are entwined with the depiction of that month's labour is a reflection of the close connection between astrology and the turning of the seasons. Living as close to nature as they did, the movement of the constellations and the rhythm of their work year would have been closely entwined in the mind and lives of the medieval labourer as well. This delightful, colourful, and sometimes whimsical illustrated page gives us an idea of the constant effort necessary for survival during this period.[3]

In spite of the technological developments such as the iron ploughshare, which allowed heavier soils to be brought under cultivation, and rotation of crops which increased agricultural production, there were still famines. This was largely because of the slim margin between survival and want. Harsh weather for one or two seasons could wreak havoc on agricultural production and tip the fragile balance from subsistence to starvation.[4]

The life of the peasant was harsh. The work of farming the land was physically demanding. He had the obligation of working part of the time for the lord of the manor, and had to pay one-tenth of his produce to the parish church.[5] His accommodation was simple; his possessions few.

For food, the peasant family would have the bounty of their own garden. This meant that there would almost always be an abundance of vegetables, according to the season, though even this was dependent on climatic conditions. The availability of meat would depend on whether the peasant was wealthy enough to have his own livestock. The primary source of meat and fat was from pigs, but beef, lamb, and chicken were also eaten if it could be afforded.[6] Almost every peasant household had chickens both to eat and for eggs. Milk was only available in the spring and summer when the calves were weaned. For that reason, it was made into butter and cheese which could be preserved and enjoyed during the year. Sometimes fish would be available from local rivers and ponds.[7]

For peasant and nobility alike, bread was the staple food, although the quality of bread eaten depended on social status. The bread of the peasant was coarse and often contained grains other than wheat, while the bread of the upper classes was more refined.[8]

Usually, members of all social classes ate two meals a day. They consisted of a large meal around noon and a lighter meal in the evening.

For all households, the preparation of the noon meal required much labour in the morning.[9]

Meals for the common labourer would differ greatly from those of the upper classes both in quality and presentation. Some peasant houses had trestle tables and benches for sitting and eating, in others the family ate from a bowl or trencher placed on their laps.[10]

The preparation of the food would of course vary depending on one's social class. Food served as a status symbol, as did the presentation of the food. For the nobility, a banquet was a way to display one's wealth and sophistication, and care was taken with every aspect of the production.

In the houses of the nobility, tables for large and festive meals were arranged in a 'U' fashion to enable the most efficient serving of the food. The lord and lady of the manor, and their honoured guests, would be seated on a raised dais. Social status was determined by the proximity to the head table, with those of high status closer, and those of lower status farther away. The table would be covered with the finest available cloth. Napkins and hand towels were also provided to encourage the diner *not* to use the tablecloth to wipe the hands.

The finest serving vessels would be displayed on the only other piece of furniture likely in the room: a serving table. On the table, the prominent container would be the salt-cellar. All of these items would be made from the finest materials and display the finest craftsmanship the host could afford. They were meant to be admired by the diners and to stimulate conversation.

The utensils on the table itself usually consisted of a spoon and trencher. The trencher was a thick slice of old bread that served as a plate. It soaked up the juices from the food (preventing them from soiling the cloth) taken from the communal bowl. After the meal, it was most often given as alms to the poor. The guest was normally expected to bring his or her own knife, which was used to spear a piece of food from the serving dish, cut meat into small pieces, and (after being wiped clean) to lift salt from the salt-cellar. What could not be eaten with the spoon was usually eaten with the fingers. For this reason, cleanliness of the hands was very important. Basins of water were presented to each guest for washing the hands both before and after the meal and between courses.

Forks were virtually unknown as eating utensils in Europe in the Middle Ages. They were introduced from Islamic lands into Byzantium, and from there to the West. An amusing story from the eleventh century illustrates the novelty of this now common eating implement:

> A Byzantine princess came to marry the future Doge, Domenico Selvo, and at one of the celebrations she scandalized society by refusing to eat with her hands like any ordinary mortal. Instead, after the food had been cut up into little pieces by her eunuchs, she fastidiously popped them one by one into her mouth with a golden fork. Total decadence. [11]

Drinking vessels ranged from a drinking horn to cups and goblets made from pewter or precious metals. Glass was not widely available, very precious if it was, and rarely used at the table.

The meal itself was usually served in two courses, but with several dishes making up each course. This would vary according to the occasion and the wealth and status of the host. The first course could consist of several meat or fish dishes, accompanied by several sweet dishes. The guests were meant to share the food in groups of two, four, or six. They also shared drinks, drinking from a common cup.

For entertainment, the guests had conversation with each other. The meal would be an opportunity to catch up on the latest gossip, comment on the food and the fancy serving vessels, and tell stories. For festive occasions there would be music or entertainment, or both.

Equally important to the food consumed to live, for peasant and noble alike, was the food for the life of the soul: the church. The church had always been the centre of life. It was the place where the community gathered for important announcements; a place of safety in times of siege; a place to pray for relief from burdens and worries

2.2 Exterior, St Sernin, Toulouse, France, 1080-1117.

both personal and communal. In a time marked by uncertainty and violence, the church was a place of refuge, a place of safety in an uncertain world.

The increased prosperity of the time allowed for the construction of larger and more ostentatious churches. Because of the importance of the church to the community, the resources of the community were utilised to build larger churches. The presence of a large and magnificent church reflected back on the prosperity and piety of the community's inhabitants.

The architecture of the churches reflected the role of church in society. The Church of St Sernin in Toulouse (pl. 2.2) demonstrates this concept. From the outside it seems to hug the ground. It gives the feeling of something durable, solid. Yet the tower over the crossing rises up and points toward heaven. It was at the same time a haven from the world and a reminder of the next world the pious Christian would enter. The exterior of the church is not highly decorated. Most of the statuary was to be found within. The church was meant to gather people inside and provide shelter for them.

2.3 Nave, St Sernin, Toulouse, France, 1080-1117.

Once inside the church, the people were treated to a majestic, vaulted space (pl. 2.3). Though the orientation of the nave is longitudinal, toward the apse and altar which was the centre of worship, the height of the stone ceiling also lifted the worshippers' eyes upward. Once inside, they were meant to leave their worldly life behind, and be lifted above worldly cares to a different plane. They entered through the west door and faced the altar positioned at the east end of the church. This was the direction where the sun rose, reflecting perfectly the Christian notion of Christ as the son of God, risen from the dead, the source of light and life.

The technological developments which allowed this structuring of space related to the arch, and the gradual understanding of the builders of the time of how to use the vaults to distribute the weight of the masonry. The builders would have been familiar with the arch, as the remains of the Roman presence from eight hundred years earlier would still have been visible. Their adoption of this structural device gives the name to the style of churches of the period: Romanesque.

Prior to this time, the roofs of churches were made of wood and/or thatch. This created a fire hazard, and when a roof caught fire, it spread quickly and the whole building could be destroyed by the wooden timbers falling into the church below. The solution to the problem was the stone vaulted ceiling. Such a ceiling provided both protection from fire and a soaring, majestic inner space for the church. A side benefit was the increased acoustic capacity of such a ceiling, which amplified the songs and chants of the monks and congregation, adding heavenly sounds to the heavenly space within the church.[12]

In order to support such a heavy ceiling, the walls had to be thick and supported from the outside by buttressing. In the process of perfecting the engineering necessary, many a builder overstepped his capacity by trying to build a vault higher than the walls could support, and the vaults collapsed.

Nevertheless, monumental churches continued to be built, spurred on by the increasing prosperity of the era. Groups of skilled masons circulated throughout Europe, sharing their knowledge and skills as they came into contact with each other. Communities competed with one another in having the largest church, the highest nave, the most sumptuously appointed church. This gave rise to the comment of one monk in the eleventh century, that the countryside was putting on a 'white mantle of churches'.[13]

In spite of the increased prosperity and improvements in the lives of some of the people, life was still harsh and short. The average life expectancy in the Middle Ages was thirty to thirty-five years.[14] The life of the peasant was especially difficult, even brutal. They worked outside much of the year where they were exposed to the elements. Food was basic and coarse. Death and disease were constant life partners.

The same Church that provided them with solace and prayers in time of need reminded them of the horrors of hell that awaited them if they did not abide by the laws of the Church.

At a time when the vast majority of people were illiterate, images served to communicate the precepts of the Church.[15] Depictions of the horror of hell awaiting those who lived sinful lives were often juxtaposed with the peace and joy awaiting those who lived their lives in accordance with the laws of the Church. In the tympanum of the Church of St Lazare in Autun, France, we see just such a scene (pl. 2.4 and detail pl. 2.4a). Christ sits immobile in the centre of the carving. On his right the blessed rise up out of their graves and ascend to the heavens, where the angels and prophets await them. On Christ's left, the devil rejoices in greedy anticipation of the souls coming to him. He reaches out to try to tip the scales in his favour, while his helpers reach out to terrorize other souls. Depictions like this were heightened in effect by the paint that has since worn off.

Paintings in manuscripts also reflect the horrors of hell. In the image of colour plate 2.5, the angel locks the door as tortured and suffering souls are pushed into the 'mouth' of hell, represented as the gaping maw of a monstrous and horrifying creature.

It is important to remember that images such as this one, and those carved in stone on the inside and outside of medieval churches, were taken very seriously by the people. They became embedded in the medieval mind. Opportunities to avoid these horrors by pilgrimage or Crusade were embraced by the populace. This contributed to the popular enthusiastic response to the call for Crusade that was shortly to come.

The Church that was so significant in the lives of the people of the Middle Ages had its own internal problems. These included the fact that the King of France, Philip I (1052-1108), was living in sin with another man's wife. Philip I imprisoned his wife and embarked on an affair with a woman who was married to a count. In spite of the fact that he was threatened with, and received, excommunication from the Church, he refused to give up the relationship. They lived together until the king's death.[16]

There was also the issue of buying and selling Church offices (simony), and secular interference in matters of the Church.[17] It was those concerns which brought the pope, Urban II, to Clermont, France, in 1095. He had called a council to discuss these matters. But

2.4 Church of St Lazare, Autun, France, by Gislebertus, 1120-1140.

2.4a Detail of 2.4, door of Church of St Lazare, Autun, Gislebertus, 1120-1140.

there was something else on his mind. He had received a delegation from the Byzantine emperor in Constantinople before leaving for this trip. The emperor had asked for his help in fighting the 'infidel', Muslim forces that were encroaching on Byzantine territory. This problem dated back to the middle of the eleventh century. A significant date was 1071, when the Byzantine army lost a battle against the Seljuk Turks at Manzikert, in modern-day Turkey.[18] This was an opening for the Muslim Turks to consolidate their gain of territory ever more deeply into Byzantine territory. This had been happening with ever greater frequency, and the emperor, Alexius I Comnenus, appealed to his co-religionists in the West for help.

Urban II was not so much interested in helping Constantinople as he was in expelling the Muslims from the holy sites of Jerusalem. The fact that the infidel was occupying the Holy City was, he felt, an insult to all Christendom. While some conflated the idea of recent Muslim encroachment on Byzantine territory with the loss of Jerusalem, in fact, the Muslims had established control of Jerusalem in the seventh century. For the most part, they had allowed Christian pilgrims to visit the city unmolested since that time. But that was not important to Urban II, and the masses of people responding to the pope's call had no idea of the history of the area.

The rallying cry for the First Crusade was to free Jerusalem and its holy sites from the hands of the infidel. In medieval Europe, it was Jerusalem that was the navel of the world and it was more a mythical than a physical location in the minds of the general populace. When Pope Urban II made his public speech at the Council of Clermont in November, 1095, he stressed the importance of Jerusalem.

> Jerusalem is the navel of the world; the land is fruitful above others, like another paradise of delights. This the Redeemer of the human race has made illustrious by His advent, has beautified by residence, has consecrated by suffering, has redeemed by death, has glorified by

> burial. This royal city, therefore, situated at the centre
> of the world, is now held captive by His enemies, and
> is in subjection to those who do not know God, to the
> worship of the heathens. She seeks therefore and desires
> to be liberated, and does not cease to implore you to
> come to her aid.[19]

Thus the throng who were moved to take the cross understood that their cause was to liberate Jerusalem. Even though the pope had mentioned it in his speech, the concept of helping the Byzantine emperor reclaim his kingdom from the Muslims did not figure large in the minds of the Crusaders. This had a significant impact on the progress of the First Crusade, as we shall see.

The importance of Jerusalem is reflected in the maps of the period. The one shown here from about 1200 (col. pl. 2.6), is based on a *mappa mundi*, a 'world map', and shows the central position of Jerusalem in the minds of the Western medieval Christians. Jerusalem was considered an earthly symbol of the spiritual world idealized into the perfect form of a circle.[20] Produced after the capture of Jerusalem, the map shows the major holy sites which every Christian visiting the city would need to see. A group of pilgrims is seen at the left border of the circle at the point where the original Crusaders broke through the walls and entered the city. They are on their way to visit these sites. At the bottom of the map, Christian Crusaders on horseback are pursuing the infidel. The forward Crusader is wearing the typical mail armour of the period and is holding a kite-shaped shield. His lance with the symbol of the cross is piercing the armour of the Muslim warrior. This scene represents the liberation of the city, the triumph of Christianity, and the power of the Cross.

The response to Pope Urban II's impassioned speech must have caught everyone by surprise. Far from appealing to just the noble class who had the training and resources to embark on a mission to fight the Muslims, the words of the pope resonated with rich and poor alike. Indeed, he stressed that both should go on Crusade. To those who took up the cause, and died in the process, the pope promised absolution and remission of sins. This was no small matter to people steeped in the images of hell that abounded in the decoration of their churches and in their consciousness.

To the very religious people of this time, the call to fight for Christ was full of gravity and meaning. Life in Europe was hard, especially for the peasant class which made up the majority of the population. There was not much reward for a life of struggle and hardship except the promise of a better life in the hereafter. But now the pope offered a new means for salvation, with the assurance that God would be pleased and would reward them for their efforts.

> Let those who have been exhausting themselves to the detriment of both body and soul now labor for a double honour. Yea, on the one hand will be the sad and poor, on the other the joyous and the wealthy; here the enemies of the Lord, there, his friends.[21]
>
> (Fulcher of Chartres)

In addition, it meant that when the peasants went on this holy war, they would go as free men, not serfs, for the lord of the manor could not prevent their leaving. Many a serf must have harboured dreams of having his own land, and of living freely in the land where Christ lived.[22]

To the younger sons of the nobility, the pope also offered new hope. These young men had been raised in the lifestyle of the manor of their fathers. But only oldest sons could inherit, and when their fathers died and the land went to their older brothers, there was nothing they could do but leave and do their best to make their own way in the world. For many of them this included terrorizing the populace, and looting the lands they passed through. This created so serious a situation, and such danger to travellers that the pope also addressed it in his speech:

> You have seen for a long time the great disorder in the
> world caused by these crimes. It is so bad in some of
> your provinces, I am told, and you are so weak in the
> administration of justice, that one can hardly go along
> the road by day or night without being attacked by
> robbers; and whether at home or abroad one is in danger
> of being despoiled whether by force or fraud.[23]
>
> (Fulcher of Chartres)

The pope felt that if these young men and their prodigious energy
could be re-directed toward a positive end, it would benefit Europe,
Christendom, and the young men themselves.

> Let those who have been accustomed unjustly to wage
> private warfare against the faithful now go against the
> infidels and end with victory this war which should have
> been begun long ago. Let those who for a long time
> have been robbers, now become knights. Let those who
> have been fighting against their brothers and relatives
> now fight in a proper way against the barbarians. Let
> those who have been serving as mercenaries for small
> pay now obtain the eternal reward … Let those who go
> not put off the journey, but rent their lands and collect
> money for their expenses; and as soon as winter is over
> and spring comes, let them eagerly set out on the way
> with God as their guide.[24]
>
> (Fulcher of Chartres)

And so, with the timeline set by the pope, heady with their
newfound freedom and sense of religious purpose, the first group
left from France in the spring of 1095. They travelled in bands
under local leaders. As they marched on, their numbers swelled
as groups merged and re-formed. Their provisions soon ran out.
There was no discipline and they were ill-prepared and ill-equipped

for such a journey. They marched through the countryside, taking food and shelter where they could find it. When they met with Jews, they slaughtered them. In almost every way, they ravaged the countryside on their way to Constantinople.[25] When they arrived there, the emperor was appalled. What was this group of rag-tag men, women and children?

When he had asked for aid from the Roman pope, he had hoped for a small, trained, and well-equipped group of knights, fighters who could beef up his forces and help him re-take the lands the Muslims had conquered. This group that he saw as he gazed out over the city walls was nothing but a nuisance. He had already received complaints from the neighbouring towns about how they had stolen provisions, looting and pillaging with no respect for the owners of the land.

If it was battle with the infidel they wanted, he would give it to them. Just across the Bosphorus, the enemy was waiting. So he helped them across the water, and left them to their fate. That fate was for masses of them to be killed by the Muslim Turks. A few made their way back to the safety of Constantinople, but the greater number perished.

The second group that left from France, Italy, and Germany, was more what the emperor had in mind, but not exactly. Four armies set off from Europe, taking four different routes to converge eventually in Constantinople (see Map 2). They came from north-western France, central France, southern France, and Italy.[26] At least these groups had spent some time preparing, and were equipped with horses and armour. Some of the leaders he had met before, and not under the best of circumstances. A group from Italy was led by Bohemond, who had tried to conquer Byzantine territory and had defeated Alexius I and his army in battle in the process.

Leaders of the other groups were unknown to the emperor, but not to each other. The French contingent was almost all related to each other. They were descendents of the Montlhéry family, and shared common grandparents.[27] Among them was Baldwin Le Bourg, Melisende's father. He travelled in the army of his cousins, Godfrey of Bouillon, and Baldwin of Boulogne, Godfrey's brother.

In addition to the nobility, who brought their own armour and were mounted on horses, were the footsoldiers, or infantrymen. Each knight had four or five men to support him. These men often became part of the group of footsoldiers associated with the campaign. These men might have had weapons of combat that they could wield by hand: spears, swords, clubs, axes and bows.[28]

The numbers of men embarking on the First Crusade has been a subject of much debate, but it is estimated that about 42,000 men made up the fighting force, including 7,000 knights and 35,000 infantry. These would have accompanied by 20,000 to 60,000 non-combatants.[29] The majority of the participants in the Crusade were not knights, but members of the middle and lower classes.[30]

The magnificence of the Byzantine court must have dazzled these men. Certainly no city in Europe was the equal of Constantinople in size, wealth, or stature. Paris in the twelfth century had fewer than 25,000 inhabitants, and was the largest town in northern Europe. Towns such as Milan, Venice, Genoa and Naples in Italy had about the same population as Paris. London was about 10,000 in population at the time.[31] In contrast, Constantinople's population numbered around 400,000 in the 1200s.[32] We can assume it was a similar size a hundred years earlier. Within the walls of the city were innumerable churches, monasteries and shrines. These were filled with mosaics, sumptuous artworks, icons, and reliquaries. It is sure that the emperor used all the means at his disposal to impress his visitors with his power and wealth.

Still, they would not be cowed by this emperor. They came, not so much to aid him as to fulfil their holy mission of recapturing Jerusalem and the Holy Land from the infidel. If they could make their own fortune on the way, so much the better. Even if they were killed, the pope had promised remission of sins and a straight path to heaven. Still, they needed the emperor's help and expertise in fighting the Turks.

The Byzantine emperor was suspicious. His experience of the first group had made him wary. He asked the leaders of the Crusade for a vow of loyalty. With the exception of Bohemond, whom he did not trust anyway, they refused. After a week or so of refusing them provisions, they reconsidered.

He called them to the palace. Each, in turn, bowed before the emperor, kissed his ring, and promised him loyalty, and the return to him of all Byzantine lands they had captured. With that assurance in hand, but still watchful, the combined forces of the Crusaders and the Byzantines set off to fight the infidel.

For the Byzantines, the goal of the expedition was to recapture lost territory. The idea of capturing Jerusalem was not an issue. To the Byzantines, their city, Constantinople, was the centre of Christianity, and their church, Hagia Sophia, the most important building of Christianity. How different was this idea from that of the Western knights!

Anxious to start their pilgrimage, the knights and their followers left Constantinople in the company of Emperor Alexius' troops. Several events that occurred on their journey shaped the kingdom and policy that Queen Melisende was to inherit.

First was the perceived treachery of the Byzantine emperor in the attempt to conquer the first city they endeavoured to take, Nicaea. The Crusaders had surrounded the city which contained a large Turkish force. When Muslim reinforcements appeared, the fighting was fierce. Caught by surprise at the size of the force and the skill of the Western knights, the Muslim warriors fought valiantly, but the Crusaders managed to make them retreat. Bolstered by their success and wanting to further intimidate the force inside the garrisoned city, the Crusading army cut off the heads of many of the enemy corpses and threw them over the walls or put them on pikes and paraded them in front of the gates (col. pl. 2.7).[33]

The styles of warfare of the Byzantines and the Crusaders were similar, but their attitude toward the enemy and the means of securing territory was quite different. The Byzantines, after many years of having lived with and fought the Muslim armies, had found that diplomacy was often a better way of dealing with them than open fighting. Over the years they had learned to live side by side with them, sometimes in peace, and sometimes in war. In the siege of Nicaea, the Byzantines made use of their years of experience with the Muslims. A further assault on the city was planned, but Alexius managed to make contact with the Turkish garrison within the city and negotiate a surrender the night before the assault was to take place. Unbeknown to the Crusaders, Alexius had achieved a diplomatic victory over the town. How surprised and outraged the Crusaders were that morning they woke up and found the Byzantine flag flying over the city they had just been besieging. Having planned to sack and loot the city as soon as they had control over it, the army felt betrayed.[34] While technically, victory had been won, the mistrust between the two groups grew. The action on the part of the emperor solidified distrust of him and the whole Byzantine Empire.

In the meantime, the two forces continued on their way. But the Crusaders too became pragmatic warriors. When it was useful to align with the Muslims, they did so. This occurred even if they were fighting fellow Crusaders. Later, in the siege of Antioch, Bohemond acted much as Alexius I had at Nicaea, dealing with the enemy in order to take the city. He succeeded only after a long siege, during which supplies for the army became non-existent, and many soldiers were starving.

While the bulk of the Crusader forces were preoccupied with besieging Antioch, a contingent marched forth with their sights on other towns of the region. One of those cities that the Crusaders conquered was Edessa, birthplace of Queen Melisende. The city's main Christian population was Armenian, which included Queen Melisende's mother, Morphia. It was the cousin of Queen Melisende's father, whose name also was Baldwin, who took control of the city. He did this by coming to the aid of the patriarch of the city, Thoros, who, having no children of his own, adopted Baldwin I as his son and heir. When Thoros was killed, Baldwin I became ruler of the city and surrounding territory. This provided the Crusaders with a much needed boost in morale, and with a secure base and source of provisions. As the rest of the Crusaders proceeded to Jerusalem, Baldwin I stayed in Edessa and held it as a buffer and supply source for the nascent Crusader state. His policies toward the Armenian inhabitants of the city and his Muslim neighbours were far-reaching: he retained control of the area himself, but allowed them to play a part in the functioning of the state.[35] This was the state and the situation into which Queen Melisende was born some years later. In this atmosphere, she absorbed the understanding that being in control did not exclude using those people of different religions and beliefs for tasks for which they were uniquely suited.

The Crusaders rapidly adapted to conditions and needs in the East. Indeed, they did so with a rapidity and thoroughness that would both amaze and appal future Crusaders coming to the region.

As the armies marched on, encountering many hardships and obstacles, from the harsh and unforgiving climate to the fierceness of the opposition and the difficulty of the geography, many of the Crusaders questioned their mission. They became discouraged and disheartened as the anticipated time of reaching the goal of Jerusalem dragged on from months to years.

In the meantime, the Muslim armies had not even begun to understand the true threat of the Crusaders. They admired the valour of the Western knights, or Franks, as they called them. But they were also preoccupied with fighting among themselves. Over the past century, a new group of Muslims had entered the land—led by the Seljuk Turks with other Turkoman groups in their train. They battled the other Muslims for control of territory and took over land belonging to local chiefs. There was not one leader behind whom the Muslims could be united. This fragmentation affected their response to the Crusaders, and as the Crusaders advanced through Muslim lands, taking control of cities and killing their inhabitants, the Muslims struggled to focus their energies against them. More even than their military might, which was considerable, or their religious zeal, which waxed and waned, the key to the success of those on the First Crusade was the complete disarray of the leaders of the Muslims. Individually powerful, their might paled in comparison to the internal conflicts which divided them. It was literally brother against brother, cousin against cousin. A general atmosphere of wariness and distrust of each other pervaded the ranks of the Muslim leaders. With this situation being perhaps their strongest ally, the Crusaders continued their march forward and fought their way to the walls of Jerusalem. In fact, after the hard fought conquest of the city of Antioch, and the decimation of surrounding towns, the Muslim rulers of the regions the Crusaders marched through rushed forward to present them with gifts and provisions in order to prevent the wholesale destruction of their own cities and lands by the conquering force.[36]

When the Crusaders finally reached the hilltop above Jerusalem and had a view of the city, it must have been an emotional experience. By that time, fully half of their number had been lost. They had arrived at this place against all odds. They had seen the glories of Constantinople, experienced what they considered the treachery of the Byzantines, weathered the harshness of the desert climate, dealt with thirst, hunger, and disease, suffered loss and deprivation, and were finally in sight of their goal.

After a two-week siege, they breached the defences and entered the city. In a fit of religious zeal, and the release of years of frustration and suffering, they slaughtered everyone in the city—every Muslim, Christian, and Jew they found, even those taking refuge in the holy places of the city. An eyewitness said the streets ran ankle-deep in blood. The rampage lasted on into the night, with the Crusaders plundering and killing the whole time.[37] This is an event given little thought or consideration by the West in the years after its occurrence, but an event indelibly imprinted on the Eastern mind.[38] Indeed, the very mention of Crusade conjures up just these kinds of images to Muslims, even of the current century. At the time it convinced the Muslims who had been watching the progress of the Crusaders that they must be driven out. Steven Runciman, often quoted in this book, says: 'It was this bloodthirsty proof of Christian fanaticism that recreated the fanaticism of Islam. When, later, wiser Latins in the East sought to find some basis on which Christian and Moslem could work together the memory of the massacre stood always in their way.'[39]

One of the primary acts of patronage of Queen Melisende was the repair and rebuilding of the most important structure to Christians in all of Jerusalem—the Church of the Holy Sepulchre. This is the church that marks the spot where it is believed that Christ was crucified. Part of the building programme of Queen Melisende and Fulk was rebuilding the double portal that serves as entrance to the south transept of the church. In the badly damaged, and hard to read lintel from the Church of the Holy Sepulchre (see below, Chapter 5), a scene with particular resonance for the Crusaders is depicted. This is the scene of the Cleansing of the Temple (John 2:13-25). From the description in the Bible, Jesus goes to Jerusalem and finds money-changers, along with people selling cattle, sheep, and doves, in the Temple. He makes a whip and drives them out of the temple and overturns the tables of the money-changers, upbraiding the perpetrators for making God's house a marketplace.

The Crusaders, far from thinking of their actions as brutal, felt justified in driving the Muslims out of Jerusalem, and considered themselves to be following Jesus' divine example by 'cleansing' the city and establishing the Kingdom of Jerusalem. The capture of the Holy City by the Crusaders on 15 July 1099 was celebrated each year. The consecration of the Holy Sepulchre was celebrated on the same day, symbolizing the link between the establishment of the kingdom and the cleansing of the new temple—the Church of the Holy Sepulchre.[40]

Misunderstanding and demonization of the 'infidel' was widely propagated in the twelfth century and beyond. Illuminated manuscripts from the time show scenes from the siege of Antioch with the Muslims throwing the severed heads of Crusaders over the ramparts at the besieging Christians. Pope Urban II, in one of the versions of his call to Crusade, refers to reports of the infidel committing atrocities against Christians in the Holy Land.

> From the confines of Jerusalem and the city of
> Constantinople a horrible tale has gone forth and very

frequently has been brought to our ears, namely, that a race from the kingdom of the Persians, an accursed race, a race utterly alienated from God, a generation forsooth which has not directed its heart and has not entrusted its spirit to God, has invaded the lands of those Christians and has depopulated them by the sword, pillage and fire; it has led away a part of the captives into its own country, and a part it has destroyed by cruel tortures; it has either entirely destroyed the churches of God or appropriated them for the rites of its own religion. They destroy the altars, after having defiled them with their uncleanness. They circumcise the Christians, and the blood of the circumcision they either spread upon the altars or pour into the vases of the baptismal font. When they wish to torture people by a base death, they perforate their navels, and dragging forth the extremity of the intestines, bind it to a stake; then with flogging they lead the victim around until the viscera having gushed forth the victim falls prostrate upon the ground. Others they bind to a post and pierce with arrows. Others they compel to extend their necks and then, attacking them with naked swords, attempt to cut through the neck with a single blow. What shall I say of the abominable rape of the women? To speak of it is worse than to be silent. ... On whom therefore is the labor of avenging these wrongs and of recovering this territory incumbent, if not upon you? You, upon whom above other nations God has conferred remarkable glory in arms, great courage, bodily activity, and strength to humble the hairy scalp of those who resist you.[41]

(Robert the Monk's account)

The account reflects the general attitude and prejudice toward Muslims. These stories would have been widely circulated during preparations for the Crusades. In fact, Muslims often treated Christians within the cities they conquered with tolerance.

Indeed, there is much evidence to suggest it was the Christians who were responsible for the most abhorrent acts of the Crusades. The Frankish chronicler Radulph of Caen, states: 'In Ma'arra our troops boiled pagan adults in cooking-pots; they impaled children on spits and devoured them grilled.'[42]

Consider the two acts of the taking of Jerusalem. The first was in 638, when the armies of caliph 'Umar ibn al-Khattab conquered the city from the Byzantines. He granted the inhabitants the preservation of their lives and property then went to visit the Christian holy places and ended up praying outside the Church of the Holy Sepulchre.[43] In contrast, the Crusaders entered the city and slaughtered virtually every man, woman and child—Christian, Jew, and Muslim alike. Even those taking refuge in the holy places of the city were not spared. It was Western chroniclers who said that the streets ran ankle deep in blood. Raymond of Aguilers gives the following exultant report:

> With the fall of Jerusalem and its towers one could see marvellous works. Some of the pagans were mercifully beheaded, others pierced by arrows plunged from towers, and yet others, tortured for a long time, were burned to death in searing flames. Piles of heads, hands and feet lay in the houses and streets, and men and knights were running to and fro over corpses.[44]

Muslim survivors who escaped had equally horrific stories of Crusaders charging through the city, plundering and killing, and sacking the holy places.[45]

But over time, Christians too learned to live with Muslims, using the objects they produced, like pottery and metalwork, as part of their everyday life. When they were not fighting with them, the Western Crusaders traded with Muslims, and taxed them. They adopted their ways, and emulated their lifestyles. Steve Runciman says that when the Crusaders came to the Holy Land, they encountered middle-class people living better than Western kings, using luxury goods like table linen, eating from gold and silver vessels, perfuming their hair and beards with scented rose water, washing their hands in beautifully decorated bowls with water poured from equally beautiful ewers. The quality of life was far superior in the East than in the West.

While the liberation of Jerusalem was the primary goal for some, the leaders of the Crusade and some knights saw the conquest of the Holy Land as an opportunity to establish themselves with lands and titles denied them in the West. Those that had the conquest of Jerusalem as an end goal, left for home in the West after recapturing the city. But while the conquest and occupation of Jerusalem was an end for some, it was but the beginning for those who chose to stay.

First, they had to decide the form of government that was to be established in the newly liberated territories. A council of bishops and lords,[46] those who had been the leaders of the different contingents of Crusaders up to the time of the conquest of Jerusalem, were chosen to make the decision. Since monarchy was the form known to them, they adopted it for use in the new kingdom. They first chose Godfrey of Bouillon, but he refused the title of king, saying that he could not bear to wear a crown as king in the city where Christ had worn a crown of thorns.[47] When he died, his brother Baldwin of Boulogne, Count of Edessa took over. He had no qualms about the title of king, and had himself crowned King Baldwin I. At that moment, the pivotal role of Queen Melisende was determined. For this one act established both a monarchy and hereditary rule. In the eyes of itself and the dominant groups of the region, the Byzantines and the Muslims, the kingdom of Jerusalem proclaimed its legitimacy and established its intention of the inheritance of power. Baldwin became King Baldwin I, and gave the territory of Edessa to his cousin, Baldwin le Bourg, Queen Melisende's father, and the future King Baldwin II.

With their numbers diminished by those who left, the remaining Crusaders had to continue to fight to hold on to the territory they had gained. The lessons and policies developed during the First Crusade gave shape to the relationships of the newly won Crusader states.

In terms of governance, the structure was similar to that which the Crusaders had left in Europe. A feudal system was established where a lord controlled certain lands which they leased to their vassals. In return for the land, the vassals were required to pay a part of their profit from the land to the lord, and provide military service in times of need.[48]

Certain things would continue to influence future rulers of the kingdom, including Melisende. The Byzantines were viewed as enemies as much as the Muslims, and there was no question of returning former Byzantine territory to the emperor. Like the Byzantines, when the Crusaders found it useful to ally with the Muslims, they did so. While holding to the faith and customs of the Western Catholic religion, the first generation of Crusaders adapted, and in some cases, adopted Eastern customs and ways of life. To the children of those first Crusaders, the Europe of their fathers would be only some place they heard about in stories. Their lives were inextricably bound up with the way of life in the East. It was, after all, the only life they had ever known.

In describing the reactions of a traveller first arriving in the Holy Land, Steven Runciman has this to say:

> When he landed at Acre of Tyre or St Symeon, the traveller found himself at once in a strange atmosphere. Beneath the feudal superstructure Outremer was an eastern land. The luxury of its life impressed and shocked Occidentals. In western Europe life was still simple and austere. Clothes were made of wool and seldom laundered. Washing facilities were few, except in some old towns where the tradition of Roman baths lingered on. Even in the greatest castle furniture was rough and utilitarian and carpets were almost unknown. Food was coarse and lacked variety, especially during the long winter months. There was little comfort and little privacy anywhere. The Frankish East made a startling contrast.

… every noble and rich bourgeois filled his town-house with similar splendour. There were carpets and damask hangings, elegantly carved and inlaid tables and coffers, spotless bed-linen and table-linen, dinner-services in gold and silver, cutlery, fine faience and even a few dishes of porcelain from the Farther East. In Antioch water was brought by aqueducts and pipes to all the great houses from the springs at Daphne. … in Jerusalem the sewerage system installed by the Romans was still in perfect order.[49]

While the viewpoint of Runciman has been tempered by more recent scholarship about life in Europe at the time, the contrast between worlds was certainly there. We have looked at the daily life of peasants and nobles in twelfth-century Europe and we can see both the truth and exaggeration in Runciman's words. Still, we can see that life in twelfth-century Europe, or more precisely, France, while perhaps not as basic and coarse as Runciman describes, was worlds away in luxury and lifestyle from that of the East.

Queen Melisende never visited the land of her father, yet her life was very much influenced by that land. Her connection was much more firmly established with the East of her mother. Her Armenian family and friends would have loomed at least as large in her life as the French side. She was born into a curious blending of East and West: privy to stories of battles and intrigues; accompanied by knights; surrounded by servants who could be Muslim or Christian; surrounded by objects of exquisite workmanship of Muslim and Byzantine origin. These factors would form her character and influence her taste.

3
RICHES AND RITUAL:
THE BYZANTINE EMPIRE

To most of the Crusaders, knowledge of the Byzantine Empire was sketchy. Their minds could scarcely encompass the breadth and scope, not only of the empire itself, but the wealth of culture and refinement that had developed through the centuries. While ritual and display were well known to the Crusaders, especially the noble class, the degree to which it was expressed by the Byzantines would have undoubtedly impressed the visitors from the west. They certainly could not have competed with clothing worn by members of the court, or the jewellery that adorned both men and women. Likewise decorative objects would have been made of rich materials and exhibited fine craftsmanship.

The capital city, Constantinople, was established by the Roman Emperor Constantine in the fourth century. He had taken control of the Roman Empire when he won a battle against his rival, Maxentius, near the Milvian Bridge. According to the tutor of Constantine's son, in a biography of Constantine written many years after the event:

> Constantine was directed in a dream to cause the heavenly sign to be delineated on the shields of his soldiers, and so to proceed to battle. He did as he had been commanded, and he marked on their shields the letter X, with a perpendicular line drawn through it and turned round the top thus P, being the cipher of Christ.[1] (X and P, chi-rho, are the first two letters of Christos in Greek.)

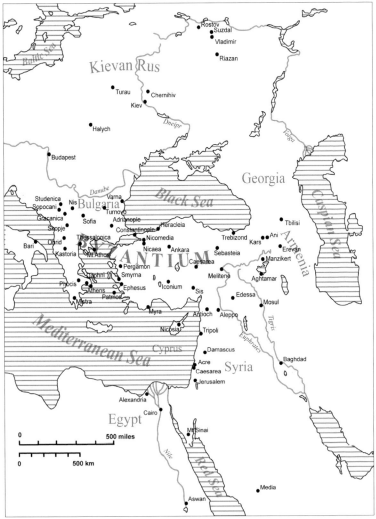

Map 3. The Byzantine Empire

The army went into battle and won. This event and the dream recorded so many years later, has been enhanced and embellished and passed into legend. However, there seems to be some basis for Constantine's religious experience, for in the next year Constantine issued the Edict of Milan, which decreed that all forms of worship would be tolerated in the empire, 'that whatsoever Divinity dwells in heaven may be favourable to us and to all those under our authority.'[2] While the Edict offered freedom of expression to all religions, it meant the most to the Christians, for they had frequently suffered persecution under previous Roman emperors.

It was a time of great unrest in the Western Roman Empire. The borders of the empire were crumbling, and Constantine wanted to establish a 'New Rome' further east. He chose a location that had great strategic advantages. A town already existed on the shores of the Bosphorus. It was called Byzantium, and was central to the trade routes of both land and sea. He named the city he founded after himself—Constantinople.[3] The people who settled there considered themselves inheritors of the greatness that was Rome and referred to themselves as Romans.[4] But they also admired and adopted the Greek heritage of the region. Over time, as the situation in Italy and the rest of the Roman Empire deteriorated, the influence of Roman culture in Constantinople declined. Greek culture and values gradually took over. In the seventh century, Greek replaced Latin as the official language at court.[5] This combination created a unique culture that was to have tremendous influence for more than eight hundred years.

The growth and development of Constantinople and the Byzantine Empire proceeded rapidly after its founding by Constantine I. Though they captured back territory in Italy from the Ostrogoths, and northern Africa from the Vandals, the Byzantine Empire's primary rival was the Persian Sasanid Empire (220-651) in the east.[6] The Byzantine contact with the Sasanians influenced many of the customs in Byzantine court life. The elaborate and showy ritual of the court of Sasanians emperors was adopted by Byzantine emperors and became an integral part of their ritual display. Artistic motifs were likewise shared between the two cultures and became an influence in Islamic art, as we will see in the next chapter.[7] Indeed, considering the wars of the Byzantines with the Persians up to the mid-seventh century, and the Muslims thereafter, we can say that the Byzantines were oriented much more to the East than the West.

By 600 the Byzantines controlled Greece, the Slavic areas north to the Danube, north Africa to Carthage, and east to Syria. After reaching its zenith in the sixth century, it then diminished in size as it lost territories in the East to the Muslims. From the middle of the ninth to the early eleventh century Byzantine armies were able to regain territory and expand the extent of the empire. By the last part of the eleventh century the empire once again contracted as the Muslim influence, led by the Seljuk Turks, encroached on Byzantine lands.[8] Even with these challenges, it is estimated that the population of Constantinople at the beginning of the thirteenth century was about 400,000,[9] making it by far the largest city in the region, and far larger than any city the Crusaders would have encountered.

In addition, the governmental institutions of the Byzantine Empire had long been established and functioning. Unlike the West, there was a comprehensive system of taxation; a trained bureaucracy to carry out the laws and government throughout the empire; a magnificent city which was not only the capital of the empire, but the religious centre of empire.[10]

When the Crusaders arrived in Constantinople, the level of wealth and sophistication there was still the envy of every other culture in the region. Even the rival Muslims recognized the greatness of the Byzantine Empire. They called the Byzantines 'Rum' from the word Roman, which the Byzantines called themselves. Al-Marwazi, an eleventh century emissary, gives this commentary:

> The Rum are a great nation. They possess extensive lands, abounding in good things. They are gifted in crafts and skilful in the fabrication of [various] articles, textiles, carpets and vessels.[11]

The importance of the Byzantine Empire and Constantinople was apparent to almost every one of the First Crusaders. Even though their aim of helping the empire was only secondary, the Crusaders needed their help in almost every way. It was the Byzantines who were familiar with the territory they would pass through on the way to Jerusalem. The Byzantines had dealt with the Muslims before, and were more familiar with their ways. The Byzantine Empire had the necessary wealth and provisions to sustain a prolonged journey through hostile territory.

The reputation for grandeur of the court and city of Constantinople must have been familiar to many of the nobles, if only through hearsay. But most of the rank and file would not have known even of the existence of such a city. There was nothing in their home countries to prepare them for the spectacles that awaited them.

Even for the nobles, the world they encountered in Constantinople as they met with the Byzantine emperor was like none they had ever seen. Fulcher of Chartres, a chronicler of the First Crusade, wrote:

> O how great is that noble and beautiful city! How many monasteries, how many palaces there are, fashioned in a wonderful way! How many wonders there are to be seen in the squares and in the different parts of [Constantinople]! I cannot bring myself to tell in detail what great masses there are of every commodity: of gold, for examples, of silver … and relics of saints.[12]

The Byzantine Empire had long been the dominant cultural and political power in the region. Over the hundreds of years of its existence, the leaders of the empire had established a complex series of ceremonies and rituals to mark every occasion. The pomp and splendour of the court was world renowned.

Fine clothes were an important statement of status and government officials were dressed in costumes of great workmanship and beauty. Every rank seemed to have its mode of dress, and the whole atmosphere was one of wealth and power. As illustrated in the image of the Archangel Michael from the pages of the Queen Melisende Psalter (col. pl. 3.1), the dress of the Byzantine emperor was widely emulated and used in art to show wealth, power, and status. The robe of the angel is modelled after that of the emperor, embroidered with gold thread and punctuated with pearls and jewels.

The Crusaders would have been treated to the most ostentatious display of power and wealth that Emperor Alexius I could muster. As with any great power the purpose was to impress and intimidate.

Anna Comnena describes how her father, Alexius I, sought to impress one of the Crusaders, his former enemy Bohemond:

> … Alexius set aside a room in the palace precincts and had the floor covered with all kinds of wealth: clothes, gold and silver coins, objects of lesser value filled the place so completely that it was impossible for anyone to walk in it. He ordered the man deputed to show Bohemond these riches to open the doors suddenly. Bohemond was amazed at the sight. 'If I had had such wealth,' he said, 'I would long ago have become master of many lands.' 'All this', said the man, 'is yours today—a present from the emperor.' Bohemond was overjoyed.[13]

Unlike the large cosmopolitan city of Constantinople, the cities of the Crusaders were much smaller, and not nearly so wealthy or well appointed. The largest cities in Europe had ten or twenty thousand inhabitants, but most of the Crusaders would have come from much smaller cities and villages. The sheer number of people in Constantinople must have been overwhelming for them.[14]

The ruler of this vast wealth and empire was the emperor. His importance and the very close relationship between him and the Church were affirmed in the art of all media throughout the Byzantine Empire. This relationship was in contrast to the situation in the West. In a fragmented Europe, the pope could not claim to be ruler of an empire, though to a greater or lesser extent throughout history, the Church controlled significant expanses of territory. As spiritual leader, he wielded power, to be sure. But his authority was often in conflict with the secular rulers, especially over issues like appointments to clerical offices and control of Church lands. Likewise there was no 'emperor' or temporal ruler who controlled any amount of territory commensurate to the Byzantine Empire. Though almost everyone in Western Europe was Christian, their secular loyalties were to individual lords who controlled their lives in a much more literal way than did the pope. But in the East, for the most part, the co-operation of empire and Church strengthened both.[15]

In the mosaic (col. pl. 3.2), from the Church of Hagia Sophia, we see the proclaiming of royal power and piety along with the establishment of Hagia Sophia and the city of Constantinople as the seat of that power and authority. In the lunette over the doorway into the inner narthex of Hagia Sophia, created in the late 9th or early 10th century, the 6th-century emperor Justinian presents the Church of St Sophia to the Virgin Mary and Child. On the right, Constantine presents the city of Constantinople. In presenting both the city itself and its most important Church to the Virgin Mary, the two emperors affirm her as their protector. Just as she accepts and protects the Son of God, she accepts and protects these two manifestations of Byzantine faith and might. Contained in this image is the concept that in the city of Constantinople, in the very church where this lunette is found, heavenly and earthly empires converge. No need to go to Jerusalem to find this synergy. The Byzantines believed it existed there, in their own city, illustrated and confirmed by this mosaic.

Images of Christ bestowing the divine blessing of royal power were echoed in illuminated manuscripts. In an illuminated page from the Gospels of John II Comnenus of about 1128, Christ is flanked by personifications of Charity as he blesses Emperor John II Comnenus and his son and heir to the throne, Alexius. In Hagia Sophia a mosaic features John II in imperial dress (colour plate 3.3). This detail is part of a larger mosaic showing the emperor and his wife Irene on either side of the Madonna. These public and private images reaffirmed to the onlookers that God and emperor had a special and intimate relationship.

Showing the emperor and his family in their sumptuous costumes was an important statement of their wealth and power. Viewers would have understood that his robe was woven of gold thread, bedecked with precious gems and pearls, and that the crown was encrusted with jewels, with strands of pearls hanging down from it. The daughter of Alexius I, Anna Comnena, described the crown: 'The imperial diadem, decked all over with pearls and stones, some encrusted, some pendant, was shaped like a half-sphere, fitting the head closely; on either side of the temples clusters of pearls and precious stones hung down, lightly touching the cheeks. This diadem constitutes a unique ornament of the emperor's dress.'[16]

When other rulers wanted to proclaim their greatness, they would have themselves portrayed in the garb of a Byzantine emperor. Stylized and identifiable as it was, it announced their greatness and pretension to power.

Other images showing the close connection between Christ and the emperors are shown on ivory plaques and coins. The gold *hyperpyron* of Alexius I (pl. 3.4), for example, has an image of Christ on one side, and an image of Alexius I on the other. While Christ wears simple

3.4 Gold hyperpyron *of Alexius I Comnenus, Byzantine, 1092-1118.*

clothing, the emperor is dressed in full imperial regalia, complete with sceptre and another symbol of the conflating of Christian and imperial power, a globe surmounted with a cross.[17]

The purpose of the elaborate ceremonials and rituals that marked the passage of days and years in the Byzantine capital was to create an image of order and stability for the empire. Some of these displays took place inside the court and were for officials and insiders only. Others involved processions that would wind through the streets of Constantinople. These were spectacles in which the onlookers could participate, if only by looking. But whether inside or outside the confines of the court, the purpose was the same: to give the impression of an empire of power and might reinforced by the regularity and harmony of its civic and religious institutions.[18]

A complex and hierarchical bureaucracy carried out the laws promulgated in Constantinople (hence 'Byzantine' to describe labyrinthine policies and departments). They collected taxes, oversaw the armies, and managed the affairs of the empire. These institutions were replicated in the outlying cities and territories of the empire. This created a need for literate and educated officials.[19] This was in stark contrast to the illiteracy so prevalent among even the nobles coming from Western countries at the time of the Crusades.

The relationship of the Church and the empire, with the emperor at its head, is reflected in the placement of the two greatest architectural symbols of each in Constantinople. The imperial palace and the cathedral complex of Hagia Sophia face each other on either side of the main square. This was meant to convey the idea of two bases of power, theoretically separate, but inextricably linked, a concept codified in Byzantine law.[20] Just as we have seen in the artwork above, the relationship between the emperor and God, and by implication, Church and state, was shown to be very intimate indeed.

To every citizen of Constantinople, if not the entire empire, the crown of Christendom was their city's Cathedral of Hagia Sophia (pl. 3.5). This is true almost literally, as the dome of the church resembles a crown. Both by its height and its position on the top of a hill, it towers

3.5 Hagia Sophia, Istanbul, Turkey, 532-537.

over the city and is visible from far and near. The people were not in need of this reminder of the importance of the church, as it permeated every aspect of their lives. Much as their Christian counterparts in the West, they marked the progression of the year by Church feasts, and there was a sacrament for every important occasion in their lives, from their baptism at birth to the last blessing at death.[21]

There was no other church in Christendom like Hagia Sophia.[22] It was built in the sixth century during the reign of Justinian I, who approved the vast outlay of public funds needed for its construction. To design this remarkable building, Justinian brought together two scientists from disparate fields who had never constructed a building. Anthemius of Tralles was a Greek mathematician, specializing in geometry and optics. Isidorus of Miletus was a professor of physics with special interest and expertise in the mechanics of thrust and support. He had also written a work on vaulting. The two men came up with a design that combined the basilica style of Roman building, and the centrally planned, dome structure which was primarily associated with martyria. In order to combine the two elements, they devised pendentives, triangular curved pieces of masonry that allow the transition from the square to the dome. This also allowed the weight of the dome to be distributed down the supporting columns to the ground.[23] Completed in only five years, Hagia Sophia became thoroughly identified with Eastern Christianity, the Byzantine Empire and the capital city where it was located.

To enter the cathedral is to understand the synthesis of Byzantine religion, art, and culture. It is the very symbol of how closely they are related. When one enters the vast space, the eyes automatically lift up and receive the magnificent sight of the dome, earthly symbol of the vault of heaven. The windows that surround the base of the dome create the feeling that the dome is floating over the space. The vastness of the structure invites a feeling of awe (pl. 3.6). The domes and semi-domes of the interior create a vast, central, rhythmic space. Like the Romanesque church, the viewer is meant to be lifted out of his or her worldly life into the life of the spirit.

The art that filled the interior originally was meant to convey the wealth and grandeur of the empire. The building was made possible by that wealth, and reflected it back for every visitor to see and enjoy. The dome was decorated with mosaics, each tiny glass piece set at an angle to reflect the light. Coloured marble panels covered the walls. The windows were of coloured glass. The columns were made of porphyry and green marble. The sanctuary screen had red drapes which set off the silver of the columns and architrave.[24] All of the colours of the materials reflected the light coming in the windows to create a magical, luminous space which was meant to aid the congregation in their worship and contemplation.

Procopius, a sixth-century witness to the wonders of Hagia Sophia, describes his experience this way:

> The vision constantly shifts suddenly, for the beholder is utterly unable to select which particular detail he should admire more than all the others. But even so,

3.6 Interior, Hagia Sophia.

> though they turn their attention to every side and look
> with contracted brows upon every detail, observers
> are still unable to understand the skilful craftsmanship,
> but they always depart from there overwhelmed by the
> bewildering sight.[25]

The special relationship of the emperor and the Church was
understood in the fact of the building itself. The glorification of God
was also the glorification of the emperor who built such a testament
to his faith and piety. He alone was able to be a part of the church
ritual.[26] His participation in it put him on equal footing with the
patriarch, and reinforced the idea of the fusion of Church and state,
God and government, and the emperor's role as ruler of both the
secular and religious realms.

Like all buildings, Hagia Sophia has a story to tell. Built as testimony
to the greatness of an emperor and the Church, all future emperors
made use of this connection. They sometimes added further testimony
to their own greatness and piety, as we saw in the mosaic lunette added in

the late ninth or tenth century. When Constantinople was conquered by the Muslims in 1453, they too put their stamp on the building. Known as one of the great architectural monuments to Christianity, one of the first acts of Mehmet II was to turn Hagia Sophia into a mosque. This act proclaimed the supplanting of one religion with another, and consolidated the rule of the new Muslim masters of the city. The building was adapted to Muslim worship by removing or covering visual Christian references and by adding the *mihrab*, *minbar*, and *maqsura* to proclaim the space as Muslim. The large roundels with Arabic script were further proof that this was Muslim space. On the outside, they added the four tall towers to serve as minarets. When President Kemal Ataturk turned the building into the Ayasofya Museum in 1935, all of the markers of its history were left in place.[27] The viewer today can read the history of the building on its face.

It is likely that, if the Crusaders attended services in Hagia Sophia, only the nobles, knights of standing, and the highest prelates would have been allowed to attend. They would have been in the company of elegantly dressed worshippers wearing their best jewellery, whose clothes and hair were scented with rosewater. Rich as some of the First Crusaders were, they could have scarcely been able to compete with the finery of their Byzantine hosts.

The Crusaders would have noted the privileged position of the emperor. In keeping with Greek Orthodox practice, much of the ritual was hidden from the view of the congregation by curtains and railings around the sanctuary. Only the emperor was allowed to stand with the patriarch of the Church during the service. They would exchange the kiss of peace, and the emperor would receive communion separately from the rest of the congregation.[28]

How shocking it would have been for any of the north European travellers to enter a Byzantine church: the interior space filled with light; the vibrant colour and sparkling surfaces of the mosaics; the height of the dome. But, most of all, the primary visual message of Christ Pantocrator (all sovereign) in the circle of the dome, His hand held up in blessing, looking down on the faithful gathered below (col. pl. 3.7).[29]

How different from the imagery in their own churches, the crucifix: Christ's body displayed on the cross, transmitting a message of suffering and sacrifice.

These two different ways of seeing and perceiving the Deity were imprinted on the mind and consciousness of the people from each of the cultures. For the Byzantine, the soaring domed church with the image of Christ as all knowing, all-pervasive, is like the emperor and the empire itself. The stylized religious ceremonies echo the order so apparent in the ceremonials of the court, giving assurance of stability and regularity in both secular and religious life.

For the Westerner, the suffering image of Christ reflected the medieval viewer's own suffering and sacrifice, and the emphasis was not on being blessed in this world, but on a life to be suffered in order to get to the next. The church offered a temporal refuge. The basilica style churches with their high stone vaults were meant to lift the worshipper out of his or her daily life, but the massive pillars and thick stone walls supporting those ceilings gave a sense of support and refuge for the worshipper which was necessary in an uncertain world.

And how different the other images! Byzantine icons of the saints: disembodied images floating on a real gold background, somewhere between the viewer and the holy space they occupied. The frames of some of these icons were encrusted with jewels, covered with gold and sometimes enamels, decorated with the finest and most delicate gold work the artist could create (col. pl. 3.8). As images with holy power, the best materials were used in their production. In addition to reflecting the religious value of the object, these stunning works of art added to the status of the owner.

The icon was one of the most important and familiar objects of veneration for Byzantine Christians. The term icon means, in this sense, a painted panel of a sacred subject intended for veneration.[30] They could be made of different materials, large or small, stationary or portable, used in communal worship in the church, or for individual worship in the home.

The goal of the artist of the icon was not to make a realistic portrait. It was to create an image that could motivate the viewer to rise above him or herself to reach a higher level of consciousness. Thus the figures are static in order to still the mind of the viewer. They were not meant to stir the emotions, but to soothe them. Much like Christ Pantocrator who presides calmly over the motions of man and the universe, the icon is the representation of a holy person's still presence in the midst of the turmoil of the life of the individual.[31]

The gold background of many of the icons was meant to catch the light of candles which were placed in front of, or around the icon. The effect of the light bouncing off the gold intensified the effect of the figure hovering in a shimmering, otherworldly space. The words of Symeon of Thessaloniki illustrate the impact: 'by seeing the saints and their beauty and through the light of the divine lights [lamps and tapers] our sight becomes bright and holy and we shine within.'[32]

Icons had a two-fold purpose: they were to make the figure or scene illustrated come alive for the viewer; and to transmit the worshipper's prayer through the image depicted to God. '… For in beholding the icon mortal man lifts his spirit to a mightier appearance, no longer distracted in veneration; engraving the image within himself he trembles at the presence. The eyes stir the depths of the soul, and by its colours art carries aloft the prayers of the mind.'[33]

We find images in illuminated manuscripts meant to mimic both the form and meaning of icons. In the example from a manuscript (col. pl. 3.9) made in Constantinople in 1133, the evangelist John stands, as if transfixed, his head turned back to the hand of God appearing from a corner of the manuscript. This reflects the belief that the gospel of John was dictated directly by God. The format closely follows that of icons, with the background of gold leaf indicating a holy space and the image suspended in that space.

Many icons were made of beautiful materials and small enough to be worn. In colour plate 3.10, the pendant icon is made of lapis lazuli, a precious stone originating in Afghanistan. It is embellished with gold filigree inlay and mounted in a gold frame. On one side is the image of Christ; on the other the standing figure of the Virgin Mary Orans (praying). Because of the exquisite nature of the workmanship and the precious nature of the material, it would have conferred status as well as blessing on the wearer.[34]

If the Crusaders had been able to attend one of the fairs of the empire, they would have encountered an incredible variety and quality of goods. A twelfth-century satirical dialogue describes the *panegyris*, a type of local or international religious and commercial fair which included markets, entertainments, and religious events. The goods offered there included 'every type … of textiles and yarns for men and women, and all those that commercial ships bring to the Hellenes from Boeotia, the Peloponnese, and Italy. And also Phoenicia contributes and Egypt, Spain, and the Pillars of Hercules weave the most beautiful textiles. Merchants bring these directly from the various lands to former Macedonia and to Thessalonike. The Euxine [Black Sea region] sends its goods to Byzantium …'[35]

While the crusaders of every rank would have attended fairs in the regions where they lived in Europe, the fairs in the Byzantine Empire, containing as they did products from places unknown to the vast majority of the Crusaders, offered new and unimagined objects to contemplate.

Consider the silk fragment from the Eastern Mediterranean (col. pl. 3.11). The bright colour, the range of animals depicted in the pearl roundels, and the other design elements present a lively and complex pattern. Scholarly discussion about the origin of this fragment points to the range of influences shown in the designs and decorative elements of this piece. Elements from Islamic, Armenian, Sasanian and Byzantine sources have been identified. In fact, the ornamentation may suggest the fragment reflects the taste and preference of the region rather than a specific culture.[36]

The blending of styles that we see in this fabric illustrates the lengthy history and shared cultural inheritance of both the Byzantines and the Muslims. Both cultures are the inheritors of Sasanian (224

-651) artistic expression.[37] The Byzantines and the Persians warred with each other, but also exchanged embassies, allowing each to be aware of the court culture of the other. Both courts made use of ceremony and the display of opulence to substantiate their importance. When the Sasanian state was conquered by Muslim forces in the seventh century, the victors absorbed both their territory and their cultural and artistic legacy. They also inherited the diplomatic structures that had existed between the Byzantines and the Sasanians which included exchange of gifts.[38] Gift-giving was an important part of diplomatic culture. These gifts were meant to impress, so they were made of the finest material and workmanship. In the following centuries, the competition and emulation of the two political powers in the region led to an exchange of artistic motifs that continued up to and beyond the time of the Crusaders' arrival in Constantinople. While the Byzantines were well aware of the world all around them, it is fair to say that their orientation, historically and culturally, was more to the East than the West.

Items such as the incense burner in plate 3.12, made of silver and gilded, must have been objects of great curiosity to the Crusaders. Made in the shape of a domed building, this beautiful object was used to perfume the air of a room. The intricate construction, metalworking techniques, and unique decoration continue to amaze and delight us.[39]

The quality of Byzantine metalwork was renowned. In objects large and small, the quality of craftsmanship was unparalleled. This small temple pendant is an example (col. pl. 3.13). It is made of gold and cloisonné enamel and was meant to be worn suspended from caps, headbands, the hair, or from the flaps of a headdress. They were worn by both men and women. The small cavity would have contained a bit of cloth soaked in aromatic oil. The stick accompanying the pendant would have been used to push the cloth into the opening in the pendant. Such an exquisite object would have been owned and worn by only the most prominent members of the court in Constantinople.[40]

3.12 Incense burner in the shape of a domed building, Byzantine, 12th century.

While the objects above are luxury objects and would have been available only to the wealthy, even everyday items available in the Byzantine Empire would have been beyond anything the rank and file of Crusaders had seen back home. While pottery of all shapes and for many different functions would have been common in Europe, the decoration and glazing styles apparent everywhere in Byzantium would not have been. A common decoration on pottery for household use in Byzantium (and much of the Near East) was *sgraffito*. The earthenware was partially covered with a pale slip layer and then coated with a transparent glaze. Patterns were then made by cutting through the slip with a sharp point or by scraping it away to reveal the darker ground.[41] These items were quite popular and available all over the Byzantine Empire.

The example in plate 3.14 might have been for display rather than everyday use. The animal portrayed is a griffin, and it is attacking a doe.

3.14 Bowl with griffin attacking a doe, Byzantine, 12th century.
(© Dumbarton Oaks, Byzantine Collection, Washington, DC)

The graceful and delicate wings of the griffin, the curve of its body and tail, and the wonderful evocation of feathers or fur on its body draw the viewer's attention and enliven the surface. The slightly more awkward and elongated body of the deer rounds out the composition. This motif of an animal gouging out the eye of its prey was well known in the Byzantine world and is seen as well in other media.[42]

Some of the finest work of Byzantine smiths is seen on *staurothekai*. These are containers for pieces of the True Cross. According to legend, the True Cross upon which Christ was crucified was found by St Helena, Constantine's mother, who made an expedition to Jerusalem in the fourth century for the express purpose of finding the Cross. After finding three crosses from the place where Christ was crucified, she identified the 'True' cross when it brought a dead man back to life.

Part of the Cross was brought back to Constantinople. Pieces of the Cross were distributed as special gifts by the emperor. These were among the most prestigious gifts which could be bestowed. Elaborate containers were made to house the holy relic. These were made of the finest materials, and fashioned by the best craftsmen.

The *staurotheke* in colour plate 3.15 is just such an example. Shown is the outer cover for the container of the pieces of the True Cross that would have been housed within. A gold border with Greek inscription outlines the enameled decoration which itself outlines and sets off the precious and semi-precious stones set in the gold of the cover. Enamels of saints punctuate this jewel encrusted border. The central enamels feature Christ in the centre flanked by John the Evangelist and the Virgin Mary (with angels), and the twelve apostles. The interior of this vessel is equally ornate, as befits the holy contents.

The wealth of holy objects, their decoration and veneration, must have been quite striking to the Crusaders. The size of Constantinople itself must have been overwhelming. The cosmopolitan nature of the city, with visitors from many lands, and the pomp and circumstance of the court must have made quite an impression.

But the Crusaders were not staying in Constantinople. Their goal was Jerusalem and the liberation of the Holy City. When the leaders of the Crusades made their vows of loyalty to the emperor and promised to return all conquered lands that had been part of the empire to him, they started on their way.

As demonstrated in the taking of Nicaea, recounted in Chapter 2, the Byzantines had developed a policy of diplomacy with Muslim states that was not condoned nor appreciated by the Western forces. The Crusaders did not understand how the Byzantines could have diplomatic relations with the enemy. They viewed it as treachery. The Byzantines, however, found diplomacy and the exchange of embassies (and prisoners) a way to avoid war.[43]

The emperor never fully trusted the Crusaders, and though he provided guidance and support, a point was reached where he left them to their own devices. That point was the siege of Antioch in 1098. The

Church as a whole had five patriarchal seats: Rome, Constantinople, Alexandria, Jerusalem, and Antioch. Antioch was controlled by the Byzantines until it was captured by Muslim forces in 1085. When the Byzantine emperor made the Crusaders vow to return to him land that he had formerly controlled and was taken from him by the Muslims, it included Antioch.[44]

The emperor's forces and the Crusaders had already parted ways by the time the Crusaders reached Antioch. After a seven-month siege, the Crusaders were able to occupy the city, but were immediately besieged themselves by Turkish forces which had come to the city's relief. The superiority of numbers of the Muslim forces convinced Emperor Alexius I that the city was bound to fall to the Muslims before he could get reinforcements there, so he declined to send help. This was viewed as treachery on the part of the Crusaders, and when they had full control of the city, they refused to return it to the emperor.[45] This seemed to confirm all the suspicions that Alexius had from the start. Relations between the two groups were never the same after that. The Crusaders went on to capture Jerusalem without the aid of Constantinople.

Emperor Alexius watched with dismay as the Crusaders continued on their way. They conquered and then kept other cities for themselves. In the end, they turned out not to help the Byzantine Empire, but to add to the instability of the region and become one more component in the complicated maze of relationships with which the emperor had to contend.

The Byzantine culture which the Crusaders had experienced during their time in Constantinople and throughout the Byzantine territories remained a formidable influence. As Robin Cormack points out: 'Byzantium was therefore increasingly encircled by hostile and rival societies, whose single common belief was that Constantinople was the centre of political and artistic success.'[46] The correlation between the two—power and art—had long prompted neighbouring societies to adopt Byzantine artistic techniques and styles in order to reflect some of the glory of Byzantium onto themselves. We will see this very thing happening in the art of Queen Melisende's court. But there were also to be other influences.

The Byzantines had a long history with the Muslim culture which surrounded them. In many ways, they were more of a known quantity than the Crusaders. For the Crusaders from northern Europe, Muslim culture was less familiar. This was about to change.

4
ENCOUNTERING THE ISLAMIC WORLD

When the Crusaders crossed the Bosphorus into what was mostly Muslim-held territory, they had little idea what to expect. Their image of Muslims and Islam itself was based on misinformation, distorted accounts, and superstition. With the exception of those Crusaders who came from Sicily and southern Italy, or were familiar with Spain, most of the multitude had never met a Muslim.

It is understandable that the Muslims had a radically different view of events as the Crusades unfolded. Concerned with internal conflicts of their own, they were not aware of the scope of the danger until well into the conflict. It was with the conquest of Jerusalem in 1099 that the true aims of the Crusaders became apparent to the Muslims. Eyewitness accounts of the atrocities perpetrated by the Franks, as they were called by the Muslims, sent a wave of fear and awareness through Muslim territory. The massacre that occurred when the Crusaders entered Jerusalem, a city sacred to Jews, Muslims, and Christians, caused a shudder to pass through Muslim lands. But even that level of awareness did not halt the internal conflicts between Muslim rulers, nor unite them in opposition to the Westerners.[1]

In the seventh century, in Arabia, Islam emerged. It was separate from Judaism and Christianity, though the first adherents were familiar with these other two religions. The revelations given to the Prophet Muhammad were held to be a completion of the earlier revelations of the prophets of Judaism and Christianity.[2] Muhammad was an Arab merchant from the city of Mecca. Mecca was an important trading centre for camel caravans coming north across the Arabian peninsula

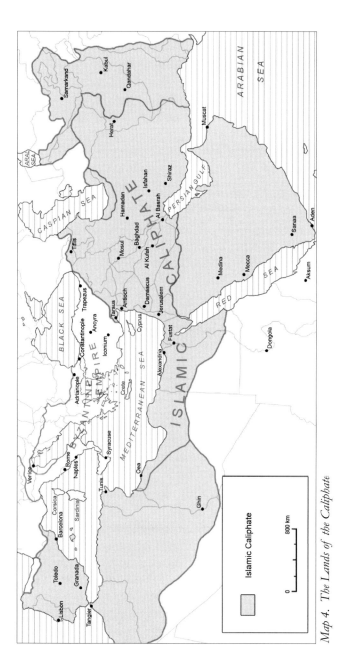

Map 4. The Lands of the Caliphate

from India, East Africa, and Yemen. These caravans were part of the trading network travelling to Byzantium and Syria with their cargo of luxury goods that included incense from the Hadramaut (in modern-day Yemen), spices and fabrics.

Muslims hold to the belief that God (Allah) revealed his message to the archangel Gabriel who transmitted it in Arabic through His Prophet, Muhammad. The revelations were recorded and collected into the sacred book of Islam, the Qur'an.[3] Written in Arabic, the language has been and remains a unifying force among Muslims, not dissimilar to Latin as a common language of Church and court in Europe during the medieval period. Because the revelations themselves were the word of God, and the language is Arabic, the language itself has an eminent position. Arabic inscriptions were often incorporated into works of art to impart a pious wish or even a blessing to the object itself, as well as to the owner and the user of the object.

Muslims believe in one all-powerful God, Allah. The religion is based on the teachings of the Qur'an and the principles called the Five Pillars. The first of the pillars is the statement of faith: there is no god but God and Muhammad is His messenger (or prophet). The other pillars are ritual worship five times a day; charity to the poor; fasting during the month of Ramadan; and, if possible, a pilgrimage to Mecca. Adherence to these five precepts identifies and defines a community of Muslims.[4]

Almost immediately after the Prophet's death in 632, internal divisions developed around the succession of leadership. In simple terms, one group felt the leader should be elected. These were the Sunnis. The other group felt the leader should be a descendant of Muhammad himself, through his son-in-law, 'Ali. These were the Shi'a. Such divisions exist today and colour the attitudes between the two main groups.[5]

The Prophet's successor was known as the caliph. He was a leader of the community, not a prophet, but the status of his office lent an air of holiness to him. He had religious and temporal authority, and he was treated with reverence and respect by Muslims.[6]

The explanation for the incredibly rapid spread of Islam is complex. The effects of plague and wars had taken its toll on the powerful civilizations controlling the area: the Byzantine Empire and the Sasanians of Persia. The decline of agriculture in the Mediterranean regions combined with the decline of demand in urban markets affected the economics of the area. In addition, the Arab forces were organized and experienced. They were motivated and united by material gain—the possibility of acquiring land and wealth. Camels were used for transporting supplies and could travel over wide areas. This adoption of traditional Bedouin techniques allowed them to move with great speed and gave them a military advantage. Their zeal and determination added to their power, making them virtually unstoppable as they moved into lands already weakened by the factors mentioned above.[7] In addition, they encountered little resistance from the local population in the conquered regions. To many of the converts, Islam was a welcome relief from the complicated theological debates within the Byzantine Church and from the heavy handedness and excessive taxation of the Byzantine Empire. The religion that Muhammad espoused, with its five pillars, found ready adherents. In little more than a century, Islam spread and was embraced by peoples from the Atlantic to the borders of China.[8] Within these areas there were still substantial numbers of non-Muslims who did not convert to the new religion, but nevertheless were under the political hegemony of the Muslims. From the death of the Prophet Muhammad in 632, Islam spread and prospered while the Western world of Europe fragmented and declined in wealth and importance.

By the tenth century, the Islamic world included much of Spain, a part of India, and extended north to beyond the Caspian Sea and south to Egypt. But this area was divided between rival caliphates: the Sunni 'Abbasid dynasty based in Baghdad, the Shi'a Fatimids of Cairo, and the Umayyad caliphate in Spain. The Umayyad/'Abbasid division dates back to the middle of the eighth century when the Damascus-based Umayyads of Syria were overthrown and replaced by the 'Abbasid dynasty, which established a new caliphate and moved their centre of power to Baghdad. The Umayyads who escaped fled to Spain and established a caliphate there. In time, Egypt and other North African areas broke away from 'Abbasid rule. The Shi'a Fatimid dynasty ruled this area and established their own caliphate based in Cairo, Egypt.[9]

In the tenth and eleventh centuries, the 'Abbasids ruled over a vast territory, but within that territory were many divisions, and the actual control the 'Abbasids were able to maintain was weak. Local rulers paid lip-service to the caliph, and welcomed his endorsement of their power, but largely maintained their own spheres of influence and control.

In the eleventh century, the 'Abbasids had to deal with a new threat—the Turks. Originally brought in as slaves and valued for their fighting ability, Turks had been familiar for generations. But at this time they came from the steppes of Central Asia to invade and take over virtual control of 'Abbasid land and government. The invasion was led by a clan called the Seljuks. The caliph still reigned in Baghdad, but he did not rule. He was a puppet of the Seljuk Turks. The group of Turks that defeated the Byzantine army at the battle of Manzikert in 1071 was led by the sultan, Alp Arslan. Thereafter, a splinter group established their own sultanate in Anatolia which they ruled independently.[10]

The Fatimid caliph in Cairo was also only a figurehead. The real power lay in the hands of the vizier. A new vizier had just come into power in 1095 after the death of the previous caliph and vizier. He was busy consolidating his power within the caliphate, which then notionally included the 'Holy Land', when the Crusaders invaded.

In the face of dissolution of centralized power, local rulers sprang up. As they fought with each other for control over territory, they contributed to the divisiveness and weakness of the Islamic world. Religious differences between the caliphates in Cairo and Baghdad further undermined any unified approach to challenge the progress of the Franks as they made their way to Jerusalem. This inability had grave repercussions for the Muslims, while at the same time creating a fortuitous opening for the Crusaders.[11]

The geographic position of Jerusalem put it between the two main warring Islamic powers. It was not of primary importance to either of them. In the years just preceding the arrival of the Crusaders, Jerusalem had been held by two Seljuk vassals. In 1097-98, the Fatimid army of the new vizier al-Afdal captured the city. When the Crusaders arrived a year later, they took the city from the Fatimids.[12]

On the eve of the Crusades Muslim lands were at odds religiously, politically, and geographically. It is probably fair to say that the internal squabbling among rival powers was of much more importance to Muslims than the arrival of the Crusaders in their territory. The Crusaders came on the same routes that Byzantine forces used, and the Muslims may not have made a distinction between these familiar adversaries and the Crusading army. When they did recognize the difference, they referred to the new invaders as *Firanji,* from 'Frank'. The term was eventually used to identify all people from Western Europe. They were also considered infidels. For Muslims, this term denoted their difference and exclusion from the Islamic world.[13]

The Muslim view of Europe and the lands of the West, if they thought of it at all, was of a place and people of distinct inferiority to themselves. They saw themselves and their own culture as being significantly more sophisticated and advanced. Their view of Christianity was also coloured by their belief that Islam was the natural continuation and perfection of Christianity, therefore superior to it.[14]

In spite of its fragmentation on the political and geographical levels, the Islamic world managed to maintain a cohesive cultural tradition. This was largely because the intellectual and cultural life of the 'Abbasids was emulated and adopted by the new rulers, even as they took over much of 'Abbasid land and power.[15] Culturally, the Islamic sphere of influence was rivalled only by the Byzantine Empire in terms of power and sophistication. The classical learning of Greece and Rome that had been kept alive in the Byzantine Empire was passed on to the Muslims.[16] By the tenth century, the Muslims had translated many Greek writings into Arabic. These texts were

1.1 Front cover, Queen Melisende Psalter, ivory.

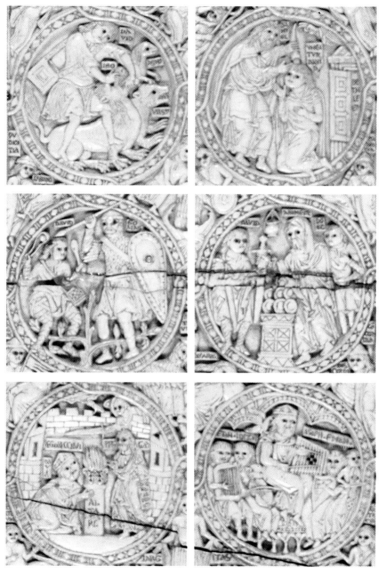

1.2 Queen Melisende Psalter, front upper cover, ivory, details.

2.1 St John's College, Cambridge, MS B.20 f.2v. Detail showing the signs of the Zodiac and labours of the months for September to December. From f.2v of MS B.20. English, 12th century.

2.5 Winchester Psalter, 1121-1161.

2.6 *Map of Jerusalem, France,* c. *1200.*

2.7 Crusaders besieging Nicaea, MS Français 2630 fol. 22v.

3.1 St Michael, Queen Melisende Psalter, 1135.

3.2 Mosaic lunette over the doorway into the inner narthex of Hagia Sophia.

3.3 John II Comnenus, Byzantine Emperor (1118-1143). Detail of the mosaic 'Madonna flanked by John Comnenus and his wife the Empress Irene'. Byzantine, c.1118-22. Istanbul, Hagia Sophia, south gallery.

3.7 Christ Pantocrator. Dome mosaic, late 11th century, Church of the Monastery at Daphni, Greece.

3.8 St Michael icon, 10th century, Treasury of the Cathedral of San Marco, Venice.

3.9 John the Evangelist, 1133. (The J Paul Getty Museum, Los Angeles, Ms. Ludwig II 4, fol. 106v. Artist unknown)

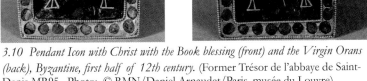

3.10 Pendant Icon with Christ with the Book blessing (front) and the Virgin Orans (back), Byzantine, first half of 12th century. (Former Trésor de l'abbaye de Saint-Denis MR95. Photo: © RMN/Daniel Arnaudet/Paris, musée du Louvre)

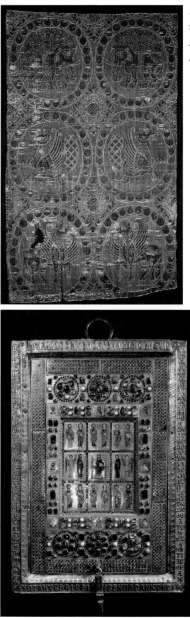

3.11 Textile with roundels of elephants, senmurvs, *and winged horses, eastern Mediterranean, Spain, 11th or 12th century.*

3.13 Temple pendant and stick, late 11th-first half of 12th century.

3.15 Reliquary of the True Cross, Byzantine, c. 955. Constantinople. Silver-gilt and enamel.

4.1 The Dome of the Rock, Jerusalem, 691.

4.2 Interior, Dome of the Rock.   *4.3 Interior, Dome of the Rock.*

4.4 Mosaics and Arabic inscriptions, interior, Dome of the Rock.

4.5 Courtyard, Great Mosque of Damascus, 706

4.6 Mosaics on exterior of prayer hall, Great Mosque of Damascus, 706.

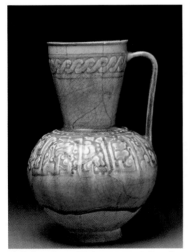

4.10 Bowl with Eagle, Fatimid, c. 1000.

4.9 Jug, Iran, 12th century. (Ashmolean Museum, University of Oxford)

4.11 Bottle. Probably Iran, about 12th century. Translucent deep green glass; mould-blown with applied decoration.

4.12 Sprinkler. Near East, possibly 12th to 13th centuries. Transparent colourless glass with greenish tinge; blown.

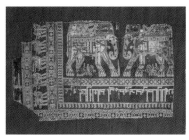

4.14 St Josse silk, Khurasan, before 960. (OA7502 © RMN/Hervé Lewandowski/Paris, musée du Louvre)

4.15 A leaf from a Qu'ran with gold kufic script on deep blue parchment, Kairouan, Tunisia. 9th century.

4.17a Cauldron (detail).

4.17 Cauldron. Made by Muhammad ibn 'Abd al-Wahid and Mas'ud ibn Ahmad al-Naqqash. Iran, Herat. 12th-early 13th century. Bronze (brass), silver and copper; cast, forged and decorated with inlay.

4.19 Banquet scene from the Maqamat *of al-Hariri, 11th c.* (Bibliothèque nationale de France)

5.8 View of Church of Holy Sepulchre from neighbouring rooftop.

5.13 Deesis, *Queen Melisende Psalter,* c. *1135.*

5.16 Lustre-painted ceramic bowl with lion, Egypt, 12th century.
(© The al-Sabah Collection, Dar al-Athar al-Islamiyyah, Kuwait)

5.14 Incipit *page,* Beatus Vir, *folio 23v, Queen Melisende Psalter, c. 1139.*

5.17 Gold wine bowl, Iran, 11th century.
(© The Trustees of the British Museum. All rights reserved)

5.18 Perfume sprinkler (qumqum). *Probably Syria; 11th-mid-13th century.*

5.19 *Bowl, Egypt, 11th-12th century.* (© The Trustees of
the British Museum. All rights reserved)

5.20 *Beaker, Syria, 12-13th c.*
(© The al-Sabah Collection, Dar al-Athar al-
Islamiyyah, Kuwait)

5.22 *Bottle. Near East,
Syria, or Egypt, Islamic,
probably 10th to 12th century.
Deep blue and opaque white
glass; blown and tooled.*

5.23 Cope with peacock motif and kufic inscription (silk embroidery), 11-12th c., St Sernin, Toulouse, France.

6.1 Griffin ewer, Mosan, c. 1150.
(© Victoria and Albert Museum, London)

6.3 St Luke, Byzantine, Constantinople, 1133. (The J Paul Getty Museum, Los Angeles, CA. ms. Ludwig II 4, fol. 69V.)

6.4 The Annunciation, Wurzberg, c. 1240. (The J Paul Getty Museum, Los Angeles, CA, ms. 4, leaf 1)

6.5 St Luke, Simone Martini, 1330s.
(The J Paul Getty Museum, Los Angeles)

6.7 Nave of San Marco, Venice.

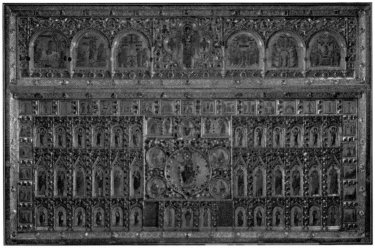

6.8 Portion of Pala d'Oro, San Marco, Venice.

6.10 Gentile da Fabriano, Madonna and Child, c. 1422.

6.11 Brass tray inlaid with silver and gold, Cairo or Damascus, 1345-6.
(© The Trustees of the British Museum. All rights reserved)

6.12 Dish, Iran, 9-10th c., St Mark's, Venice.

6.16 Islamic bottle with Christian scenes, Syria, mid-13th c.; H. 28.2 cm, max. diam. 17.8 cm

6.17 Triptych from Stavelot, c. 1155-58, *Byzantine.*

6.23 The Somerset House Conference. (© National Portrait Gallery, London)

6.24 Detail of Anatolian carpet in the painting in 6.23, artist unknown, 1604. (© National Portrait Gallery, London)

6.25 Ceiling of the Room of the Horses, Giulio Romano and assistants, c. *1530, Mantua, Palazzo del Te.*

6.28 Textile fragment with senmurvs, *Byzantine, 9-10th century.*
(Photo: Hugo Maertens. © Royal Museums of Art and History, Brussels)

6.29 Textile fragment with senmurvs, *11th or 12th century, Eastern Mediterranean. See also col. pl. 3.11.*

studied, commentaries were made, and they were developed further. In government too, the Muslims initially followed Byzantine precedent in former Byzantine lands. Rather than abolishing Byzantine political, administrative and economic structures within the old Byzantine regions, the Muslims adopted and adapted them.[17]

In their artistic tradition, the Muslims were the inheritors of the artistic legacy of the Sasanians (224-651). So too were the Byzantines, as the conflict between those two cultures brought them into close contact. Thus we see the similarity of artistic motifs such as rulers engaged in hunting and feasting, the use of vine scrolls and vegetal decoration, beaded decorative borders, and the use of mythical beasts in fabric and metalwork.[18]

The Muslims characterized Europe and Europeans according to the geographic area in which they lived. This idea was based on the works of Ptolemy, the Greek scholar of the second century whose works had been translated by Muslim scholars. According to this conception, the world was divided into different climatic zones. The zone of Europe was a place of cold and damp which affected the culture and characteristics of those who lived there. A Muslim writer of the tenth century, al-Mas'udi, describes the zone of the Franks:

> As regards the people of the northern quadrant, they are the ones for whom the sun is distant from the zenith, those who penetrate to the North, such as the Slave, the Franks, and those nations that are their neighbours. The power of the sun is weak among them because of their distance from it; cold and damp prevail in their regions, and snow and ice follow one another in endless succession. The warm humour is lacking among them; their bodies are large, their natures gross, their manners harsh, their understanding dull, and their tongues heavy. Their colour is so excessively white that it passes from white to blue; their skin is thin and their flesh thick. Their eyes are also blue, matching the character of their colouring; their hair is

lank and reddish because of the prevalence of damp mists. Their religious beliefs lack solidity, and this is because of the nature of cold and the lack of warmth.[19]

By the time of the Crusades, this stereotype of the nature of the Franks was embedded in Muslim thinking and attitudes. It was combined with the attitude that the Franks were dirty and uncouth. The superiority of Muslims and baseness of the Franks is illustrated in this one quote from Usama ibn Munqidh, who lived during the twelfth century and recorded his observations and experiences with the Crusaders. While the author was more concerned with amusing his audience than being accurate in his statements, his words do convey a sense of what Muslims thought about the Franks and illustrate the deep-seated prejudices that were in place.

> Mysterious are the works of the Creator, the author of all things! When one comes to recount cases regarding the Franks, he cannot but glorify Allah (exalted is He!) and sanctify him, for he sees them as animals *(baha'im)* possessing the virtues of courage and fighting, nothing else; just as animals have only the virtues of strength and carrying loads.[20]

This reputation was reinforced by the horrifying experience of the Muslims at the hands of the Crusaders in Ma'arra. It happened shortly after their victory in Antioch, in 1098. When the Crusaders besieged the city, and when they entered it, they spent three days killing the inhabitants. This would have been bad enough, but it was what happened afterward that makes one shrink in horror, even today. According to the Crusaders themselves: 'In Ma'arra our troops boiled pagan adults in cooking-pots; they impaled children on spits and devoured them grilled.' (Radulph of Caen); 'A terrible famine racked the army in Ma'arra, and placed it in the cruel necessity of feeding itself upon the bodies of the Saracens' (from an official letter to the pope by Crusader commanders); 'Not only did our troops not shrink from eating dead Turks and Saracens; they also ate dogs!' (Albert of Aix).[21] The Crusaders dismantled the walls of the city, burned all the houses, and went on their way, leaving the sickening memory of Ma'arra burning in the minds of local Muslims. While the Muslims had been accused of similar atrocities by the Crusaders, we have no first-hand accounts from the actual perpetrators, and the events at Ma'arra remain in a category by themselves.

As the Crusades and the Crusaders progressed to take over other cities from Muslim rulers, there were additional factors which came to underlie the hostility and mistrust of the Crusaders by the Muslims. Chief among these was the concept of defilement. To the Muslims, this concept represented separation from God. When the Crusaders took over Muslim religious buildings, such as the al-Aqsa Mosque and the Dome of the Rock in Jerusalem, they defiled them by putting crosses on the top (as with the Dome of the Rock), and superimposing their religious features on Muslim holy space.[22] This triggered the same hostility in Muslims as it had triggered in Christians when the Muslims conquered Jerusalem, and especially when al-Hakim destroyed the Church of the Holy Sepulchre in 1009. It is true that all conquering powers take over the religious structures of their predecessors and make them their own in order to proclaim their power and primacy over the old regime. But in light of the strong association between defilement and Muslim religion and belief, such acts continued to rankle and resonate with the people.

The Crusaders who managed to survive to see the Holy City must have been moved when they stopped at the top of a hill overlooking Jerusalem. As they viewed the object of their long and treacherous journey, it is said they fell on their knees and prayed. They named the hill Montjoie, the Hill of Joy.[23]

All the more significant is that the dominant building they must have seen was not a Christian site, but the Muslim Dome of the Rock (col. pl. 4.1). Its copper dome, which gleamed in the sunlight, and prominent location on a raised platform in the middle of the city stand out, even to the viewer today. The Church of the Holy Sepulchre, that most holy of Christian shrines, lies in an area crowded with other buildings, and would not have been as noticeable as the Dome of the Rock.

The Muslims had conquered Jerusalem in 638 and almost immediately built the great shrine to the Prophet's heavenly 'Night Journey' from the Dome of the Rock, to proclaim the new religion and emphasise the new power in the region. The building was completed in 691. This domed structure was a physical and symbolic response to Byzantine power and the great Hagia Sophia in Constantinople. It echoes the shape and function of other Christian buildings found in Jerusalem: the Church of the Ascension, the tomb of the Virgin Mary, and the Church of the Holy Sepulchre.

All of these Christian edifices were commemorative in nature: the Church of the Ascension commemorating the place of Christ's ascension into heaven, the tomb of the Virgin Mary where she was buried,[24] and the Church of the Holy Sepulchre commemorating where Christ was crucified. These structures were designed to accommodate pilgrims and so had a central area of the commemorative location, and an ambulatory round which the pilgrims could walk as they circulated through the shrine. The interior plan of the Dome of the Rock is similar to these other buildings. It also competes with the primary Christian place of pilgrimage in all Jerusalem, the Church of the Holy Sepulchre, by having a dome just slightly larger.[25] It is one of the oldest surviving Islamic buildings.

The Dome of the Rock was built in a commanding location on a hill where the Temple of Solomon was believed to have been built. A Muslim chronicler, al-Maqdisi, describes his reaction to the sight of the building:

> The dome, although gigantic, is covered with golden copper…Under the rising sun, the dome lights up and the drum sparkles marvellously … I have never seen in Islam anything comparable to this dome nor have I

discovered that [something comparable to] it exists in the [lands of the] infidels.[26]

The Muslims built the Dome around a rock which had important associations for Jews and Christians, as well as Muslims. The rock was believed to be the site of the creation of Adam; the place where Abraham nearly sacrificed Isaac; and the place from which Muhammad ascended to the presence of God on the Night Journey mentioned in Surah 17 of the Qur'an (col. pl. 4.2).[27]

The plan of the Dome of the Rock is octagonal. The central dome is placed right over the rock, and is supported by an arcade (col. pl. 4.3). The profusion of mosaics creates a sparkling effect that evokes the shimmering pathway that led Muhammad on his journey to heaven. Two concentric aisles allow circulation around the centre space.

The interior decoration is impressive with its complex programme of design and colour. A mosaic frieze with the earliest written text of the Qur'an goes around the inner wall. Elaborate floral motifs and vine scrolls, jewelled plants, and chalices decorate the walls (col. pl. 4.4). It is thought that some of these decorations symbolize Muslim victories, or perhaps the garden of Paradise itself. The use of mosaic decoration in such profusion was a conscious challenge and statement of superiority over Byzantine churches, for none of them had such rich decoration in this medium so closely associated with the Byzantine Empire and Church. [28]

The Arabic inscriptions, which are meant to be read as the viewer walks around the dome, emphasize the basic tenets of Islam. The references to Muhammad as the supreme prophet and warnings against the error of the Christian Trinity may have been both statements of Islamic power and lessons for recent converts.[29]

What catches the viewers eye when entering the shrine is not the display of images, but the display of forms. The style of decoration established by the embellishment of the interior of the Dome of the Rock persisted in Islamic art in all media. The use of floral and vegetal motifs, devoid of human or animal figures, continued to be used for the majority of Islamic religious buildings and objects. Likewise, the decorative use of Arabic script was to develop and permeate all types of Islamic artistic expression.

Just as the original building of the Dome of the Rock was meant to be a symbolic act of victory and power, the occupation of the building by the Crusaders made the same statement. The shrine became the Templum Domini, and was used as a church symbolized by adding a cross on the dome.

The Dome of the Rock was a shrine for pilgrims. It differs from the place where Muslims gather for communal worship, the mosque. One of the first buildings adapted to serve as a mosque was the Great Mosque of Damascus. It was built between 706 and 715 by al-Walid I, the Umayyad caliph and the son of the builder of the Dome of the Rock. The building had originally been a Roman temple dedicated to the god Jupiter. During Byzantine control of Damascus, it became a Christian church dedicated to St John the Baptist. After negotiating with the Christians, al-Walid destroyed the church and adapted the architectural framework to accommodate the needs of the Muslim worshippers. [30]

Al-Walid I kept the shape of the original Roman temple, which was a basilica style. He arranged the interior space so that the open space was parallel to the *qibla* wall, thus orienting the building and the worshippers inside toward Mecca. Outside is a courtyard (col. pl. 4.5). There is a fountain where worshippers perform the ablutions required before going into the mosque to pray.

Mosaics originally covered both the inside and outside walls of the mosque. The interior tiles were destroyed by a fire in the nineteenth century, but the outside decoration remains.[31] The western wall of the courtyard has mosaics depicting landscapes and buildings (col. pl. 4.6). There is little left of the original marble panelling on the lower part of the walls.

Mixed in with the vegetal forms and tall trees are buildings of all shapes and sizes. The gold background gives these scenes an otherworldly feeling. Because this type of decoration is unique and was not continued in other building decoration after this time, there have been many explanations about its meaning. Some scholars believe the buildings signify cities conquered by the Umayyads. Others think they could be depicting an idealized 'city of God', or the Muslim paradise mentioned in the Qur'an. Coming barely twenty years after the mosaics on the Dome of the Rock, they could reflect the new-found security of the Muslim Empire.[32]

Mosques have many different plans, but they share certain characteristics in common. The first mosques were patterned after the compound of the Prophet Muhammad, which had a courtyard and a covered area large enough to accommodate a large number of worshippers. Later, minarets might be added for the call to prayer by the muezzin. Because of their height and prominence, minarets served another purpose, and that was to proclaim Muslim dominance in a city, and indicate to visitors that they had entered a Muslim city.

Inside the mosques, worshippers sit in rows facing Mecca. The *mihrab* niche on the *qibla* wall, indicated the direction of prayer. The *mihrab* was often highly decorated. Its origin is unclear but it may have precedents in Roman temples as the focus for the statue of the god, and in the apse of Christian churches (pl. 4.7).[33]

The Near East was the focus for the major trade routes of the world and products from all over the Mediterranean, Africa, and as far as Central Asia passed through and were widely available in Muslim lands.[34] Within Islamic lands, the absence of trade barriers and regulations contributed to the ability of merchants to procure a great variety of objects from different artistic and cultural traditions. These could be seen in the market stalls in the cities, and in the homes and palaces of residents. Islamic pottery, glass, metalwork, and textiles were renowned for their high quality.

Partly spurred by the prohibition of figures in religious art, Islamic craftsmen delighted in surface decoration and developed an extensive artistic vocabulary of non-figural ornamentation. This often resulted in an almost obsessive tendency to cover every bit of surface of an object. This is known as *horror-vacuii*, the fear of empty space. Spaces

4.7 Qibla wall with mihrab and minbar, Sultan Hasan madrasa-mausoleum-mosque, Cairo, Egypt, 1356-1363.

were often filled with complex geometric designs or vegetal designs such as scrolling vines.

The use of Arabic script in the decorative arts illustrates how

4.8 Bowl with Kufic script, Samarkand, 11-12th c. (AA96 © RMN/Thierry Ollivier/Paris, musée du Louvre)

artists recognized and exploited the artistic qualities associated with Arabic as a written language. The appearance of pious Arabic phrases on an object often lent it an element of holiness. The use of Arabic script was thought by some to have a magical and protective quality as well.[35] However, many objects contain inscriptions of proverbs and adages and are of a purely secular nature. The angular style of the calligraphy on the object in plate 4.8 is called kufic, named after the city of Kufa in Iraq. The style is well suited to epigraphic uses, and appears on many objects.

The white ground of this piece imitated prized Chinese porcelains made of fine white kaolin clay. Samarkand, where this piece was made, was connected to the trade routes to China and was influenced by Chinese culture. By referencing the prized porcelain from the East, and inscribing it with decorative Arabic script, the potter makes a statement of Muslim status for the owner. The inscription reads: 'Knowledge: its taste is bitter at first, but in the end sweeter than honey. Good health [to the owner].'[36] The formal, yet rhythmic, quality of the decoration gives the bowl an elegance and sense of refinement the owner must have found quite pleasing. The harmony between the form of the object and the simple, clean lines of the decoration demonstrates the level of sophistication of objects made in Muslim lands. This bowl, and others like it, seem to have been meant for educated, urban patrons, and may have been used for purely decorative purposes.[37]

The jug in colour plate 4.9, made in Iran in the twelfth century, was also meant to imitate Chinese porcelain. It shows how the Islamic potter adopted the Chinese model, then adapted it to his client's taste. In the stylized design around the body of the jug, we again find decorative Arabic kufic script. Part of it is illegible, but we can read the words for 'glory' and 'prosperity'. The fact that the rest is not legible indicates that the potter may have been illiterate. We do not know if the buyer of this utilitarian vessel would have also been illiterate, or if he or she cared. The presence of the Arabic script in itself gave a certain sense, if not of holiness, then at least of good wishes from the maker to the recipient.[38]

Islamic ceramics made for a wealthy clientele would often be made of lustreware (col. pl. 4.10). This was a glazing technique involving two firings that produced a metallic effect. The technique originated in Iraq in the ninth century, and became very popular in the tenth to the twelfth centuries in Fatimid Egypt. These objects were meant to imitate more expensive metal objects. The sheen of the glaze creates a reflective surface. For those Muslims wary of the ostentation of gold and silver vessels, lustreware would have constituted a suitable and beautiful alternative.

There is no question that the Crusaders would have been impressed and delighted at the wealth and variety of glass objects available in the lands they passed through. There were pitchers, bottles, beakers, sprinklers, and bowls. Such vessels, both utilitarian and for show, were probably inexpensive as well as plentiful.

The glass bottle shown in colour plate 4.11 is likely to be from Iran and from the twelfth century. It was made in two sections from a mould into which the molten glass was blown. The design around the base of the neck was applied after the two sections were fused together.

Like the ceramic pieces we have seen, the bottle also has a kufic inscription. It reads: 'And to the owner happiness, and blessing, and joy.' Since the greeting is generic in nature, it indicates this bottle was intended for sale and produced in large numbers.[39]

Sprinklers were used to apply scented oil to the hair, beards, and clothing of the individual. They were used by both men and women. The essence of the scent would have been quite expensive, and a small amount of it was mixed with oil and put in the sprinklers. When shaken, a small amount of the scented oil would come out.

The sprinkler in colour plate 4.12 was made of blown, clear glass. Made in Egypt or western Asia, perhaps in the twelfth or thirteenth century, it is typical of the type of sprinkler that was widely available at the time. A sprinkler such as this would have been within the means of almost anyone, and shows the widespread use of such vessels.[40]

Sprinklers could also be made of metal. These would be used and displayed as luxury objects. The one shown in plate 4.13 is believed to have been used for rosewater which was used in a similar way to scented oil; for perfuming the hair, clothes, carpets, and also for flavouring foods. The rose was a favourite Muslim flower and the distillation of rose petals to make attar of roses is a testament to Muslim skills in chemistry.

This beautiful example has scenes in medallions around the body with additional designs between the medallions and on the neck of the sprinkler.[41]

Textiles had long been a specialty of the Islamic world. Silk fabric was light and easy to transport. Cloth was used as gifts and could even be used as currency. 'Robes of Honour' were given to officials in much the same way that medals are given for outstanding service today.[42] Workshops were often sponsored by the government, and it is not uncommon to see pieces extolling the virtues of the ruler in kufic script.

This piece in colour plate 4.14 shows two affronted elephants with small dragons between their legs. The elephants with their elaborate, woven coverings, were imported from India and used in the Samanid

4.13 Silver sprinkler with cap, early 12th century. (Freer Gallery of Art, Smithsonian Institution, Washington, D.C: Purchase, F1950.5)

army. The Samanids were one of the earliest independent dynasties in Iran, with their territory extending from eastern Iran to Central Asia (819-1005).[43] An unseen border of this piece has Bactrian camels. The inscription reads: 'Glory and prosperity to the qa'id Abu Mansur Bukhtegin, may God prolong (His favours to him?).' It was produced in Khurasan before 961.[44]

Widely used, not only for clothing, but for interior hangings to both adorn and divide living spaces, Islamic textiles were renowned far and wide. As wall hangings, they could be changed seasonally or as an occasion demanded, thus altering the interior space. Since wood was not commonly used for interior furnishings because of its scarcity, rugs and mats substituted for sitting and eating areas.[45] People sat on the floor and/or reclined on cushions. Furniture was not required for room usage and was based on seasons, with living outside usual in the warm season. The portable nature of rugs and cushions allowed them to be used inside or out.

Other items that might be found in the Islamic household were metal objects like lampstands, lanterns, and trays on wooden or metal supports. These last were also portable and could be moved around the house as needed. In the kitchen, metal items like jugs, ewers, pans, and dishes were used.[46]

The importance and significance of Arabic writing has been alluded to in prior works of art. Calligraphy was considered a very high form of artistic expression and the writing and decorating of illuminated Qur'ans provided a major source of employment for Islamic artists.[47] Because figural representation is forbidden in Islamic religious art, but less so in public, secular art, the development of decorative Arabic script flourished.

There is a treatise on calligraphy written by a famous man of letters in the early eleventh century. In it, he gives direction to the calligrapher about how to prepare a reed pen, form letters, how to take care of his hands, and even the necessity of taking a nap. He compares calligraphy to music, and the scribe to a musician. Referring to the high regard and status of the calligrapher, he says, 'In his craft he proceeds with the finest degree of sensitivity possible in sensory perception that associated with a fine soul.'[48]

In the beautiful example of a Qur'an in colour plate 4.15, probably made in the ninth century in Tunisia (or Spain as some scholars believe), we see the decorative and rhythmic possibilities of Arabic. The Qur'an has 114 chapters or *suras* with varying number of verses. The verses were chanted, and sometimes one can feel the rhythm of the words just by looking at the way they are written on the parchment.

The striking appearance of the gold ink on the deep blue parchment gives a regal character to this page. Blue was considered a

*4.16 Fatimid
ivory plaque, 11th-
12th c.*
(bpk/Museum für
Islamische Kunst,
Staatliche Museen
zu Berlin/Georg
Niedermeiser)

royal colour, and sometimes Byzantine royal documents were made of vellum that was dyed blue.[49] This Qur'an might have been imitating and competing with that tradition.

Scientific treatises, illustrated histories, and works of literature were also widely available. In the eighth century, Arabs learned paper making from Chinese prisoners. After the mid-tenth century, many Qur'ans and other books were made of paper. This made them much cheaper to produce and more accessible to a greater cross-section of the population.[50]

The ivory plaque pictured in plate 4.16 was probably part of a book frame. The seated figure is pouring wine from a flask into a cup. He is being entertained by musicians playing the flute and the lute. The figures are surrounded and encircled by grape vines, which also alludes to the wine being enjoyed. The plaque communicates a feeling of the wealthy man or ruler enjoying himself, and may indicate the prevalence and importance of music in courtly life.[51] Ivory was an expensive and precious commodity. Intricately carved ivory caskets (small boxes) were used by the wealthy. Ivory was also used for inlay in wood for furniture and panelling.

Muslim craftsmen working in metal were highly skilled. Because metals are prone to be melted down in times of economic distress, we have only a fraction of the number of objects that would have been available at the time of the Crusades. We have already seen glass and ceramic objects that would have been cheaper alternatives to those same objects made of metal. In addition to vessels for eating and drinking, there were metal caskets, bowls, penboxes, buckets, incense burners, trays and mirrors, to name just a few.[52]

Most of these objects were made of brass or bronze. It is sure that these same objects were made of the more precious metals of gold and silver, but few of these remain. In the middle of the twelfth century, objects started to be made of brass with inlays of silver and copper. This produced a lively effect and enabled designs to be more clearly seen. Such an object is the 'Bobrinski bucket' (col. pl. 4.17), made in 1163 in Herat an area which is now western Afghanistan.[53]

This small (18 cm. high), richly decorated bucket, or cauldron, was made for a merchant who is extolled in the inscription: 'pride of the merchants, the most trustworthy of the faithful, grace of the pilgrimage and the two shrines, Rashid al-Din 'Aziz ibn Abu al-Husain al-Zanjani, may his glory last.'[54] It may have been made for use in ritual ablutions during the *hajj*, the pilgrimage to Mecca.[55] These buckets were also used in public baths, and this example, decorative as it is, would have garnered a lot of attention for its owner.

Scenes of leisure pursuits, including groups of revellers, a hunting party, and a depiction of two people playing backgammon are arranged in bands around the bucket (col. pl. 4.17a). The use of animals as integral parts of the handles of the bucket contributes to the rhythm and playful quality of the work.

The artist has integrated script with playful, anthropomorphic details added by chasing. This makes the piece 'speak' to the viewer in more ways than one.

The ability to use Arabic script in this whimsical way is in keeping with the tradition of exploring and exploiting the artistic and expressive qualities of Arabic. The emphasis on surface ornamentation makes the bucket compelling in a purely visual and delightful way.

There is probably no object that better epitomizes the difference in wealth and sophistication between the Western world and the East than the combination fork and spoon shown in plate 4.18. Made in Iran in the twelfth century, the small, portable eating utensil is a masterwork of design and creativity. 14.8 cm long (slightly less than six inches), it is hinged at both ends so that the tines of the fork and the bowl of the spoon can be collapsed against the handle. Such an object would have fit neatly in one's pocket or pouch. Highly decorated, it is cast of silver, engraved, and inlaid with niello (a shiny black material made from metallic sulphides) to highlight the details. In the bowl of the spoon are Arabic inscriptions written in kufic. The phrases are: 'Power is God's, sovereignty is God's, thanks is God's, greatness is God's, glory is God's, reverence is God's.' The central medallion of the spoon is engraved with a bird,

4.18 Inlaid silver spoon and fork, front and back. Iran, 12th century.
(© The al-Sabah Collection, Dar al-Athar al-Islamiyyah, Kuwait)

and in the roundel between the spoon and fork is a winged lion. The engraved designs are also found in ceramics and textiles of the time.[56]

At a time when Europeans of all classes were eating with only a spoon and knife, the fork was not only unimaginable but unheard of. This refined and ingenious tool stands out as a masterpiece of ingenuity and craftsmanship.

How common such an eating tool was is a source of some contention, but it is clear that the sophistication of the food and habits of the Islamic population is echoed by this object.

The importance of food in Islam is confirmed by the number of cookbooks known from the Middle Ages. Lilia Zaouali states that in the years before 1400, more cookbooks in Arabic were produced that in the rest of the world's languages put together.[57] Books of recipes were compiled in Baghdad from the eighth century onward. Perhaps the most famous one was the cookbook the *Kitab al-tabikh,* set down in the tenth century by Ibn Sayyar al-Warraq.[58] The author presents recipes, includes an inventory of foods, discusses their dietary properties, and talks about rules of hygiene for both cooking equipment and cook. The comprehensive nature of this book is illustrated by his words from the introduction:

> You ordered me—may God grant you long life—to write a book in which I was to put together dishes cooked for kings, for caliphs, for lords, and for chiefs. Thus I wrote for you—may God grant you long life—an honest, complete, and elegant book that treats of the benefits of food for the body and the harm [it may possibly cause]; treats of all roasted meats and dishes cooked with meat, … all the cold appetizers of feathered game and freshwater fish, after having consulted—may God sustain you—books of ancient philosophy, and the texts of wise men.[59]

From the recipes in these books we know the great care that was taken to prepare food that appeals to not only the palate, but also the other senses. The fragrance of a dish was of utmost importance, and the spices used to produce the taste and smells that characterized the dish were an essential part of every kitchen. In many cases, the spices also produced the colours that would enhance the appearance of the food.[60]

Because meals were eaten mostly with the hands, keeping them clean was very important. Special soaps and powders were provided to the diner for this purpose. After washing, the diners would sit at a low table or on a cloth spread on the ground (see col. pl. 4.19). The dishes would be served in groups all at once, according to preference. They would include fruit, meat dishes, vegetables, and bread. Sweets were presented at the conclusion of the meal along with lozenges made from spices to prevent bad breath.

It was not the method of eating that the Franks settling in the Levant would emulate, but the food itself. Its lightness and flavour was in stark contrast with the food known to the First Crusaders and later pilgrims and Crusaders from Europe. It makes sense that the food in the East also suited the climate. Eating local food was not a difficult transition for the Westerners to make. The same taste that enchanted and delighted the Crusaders was embraced by all of Europe as well. The foods and spices imported from the East during the eleventh and twelfth centuries continue to make a big impact on Western cooking to this day.

As illustrated in this chapter and the ones preceding it, the world into which Queen Melisende was born was rich and varied in its attitudes, luxury objects, food and clothing. Because she was exposed to a myriad of cultures and practices from an early age, it must have been entirely natural to her to incorporate all these influences into her daily life, and eventually, into life in her court.

5

POWER AND PATRONAGE

With the background of the previous chapters in mind, we come now to the queen herself. One longs to have a portrait of her, her image on a coin perhaps. But alas, portraiture in the sense that we think of it had not been developed yet, and coins struck in the name of the Kingdom of Jerusalem had been minted for only a short time, and did not yet reflect the continuity of rule that Queen Melisende would ensure. We are left with the scant information about her recorded by William of Tyre and a very few others. In the turmoil in which the Crusader states were always embroiled, and especially that which followed the death of her grandson Baldwin IV and the loss of Jerusalem to Saladin in 1187, her legacy was lost. As memories of the 200-year-old Crusader states faded, and male historians interpreted the events and people of the period, Queen Melisende and her rule were buried as effectively as her body was when she died in 1161.

Even that story is telling of the attitudes of the time. The first kings of Jerusalem, Baldwin I and II, were buried in the Church of the Holy Sepulchre. When Queen Melisende died, it was deemed fit to bury her in the resting place of her mother, Morphia, close to the supposed tomb of the Virgin Mary in the Valley of the Jehosaphat. Kings can be buried near the burial place of Christ, and for queens it was considered appropriate for them to be buried close to the tomb of the Mother of Christ, Mary. This was no small honour, for the Virgin Mary was much revered in the Middle Ages. Yet it says something too that it was the Church of the Holy Sepulchre that served as the primary pilgrimage site. While the tomb of the Virgin would also have

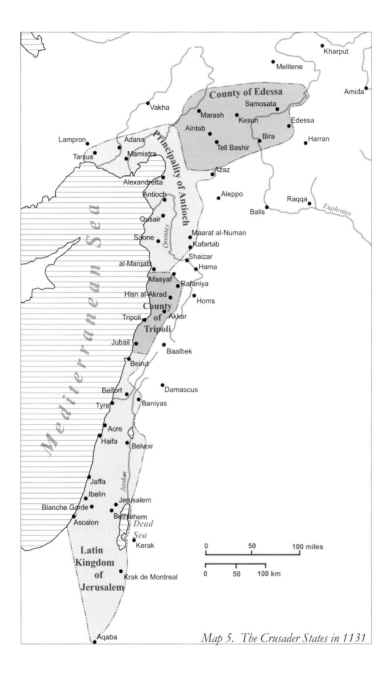

Map 5. *The Crusader States in 1131*

been among the sites visited by pilgrims, it did not have the religious or political cachet of the tomb of Christ.

It is consistent with the treatment of Queen Melisende in history that if, today, one went looking for her tomb, one would be hard put to find it. In fact, she is buried at the site of the tomb of the Virgin Mary, in a niche to the right as one descends the stairs into the dank (and sometimes flooded) cavern celebrated then and today as the tomb of the Virgin Mary. There is no marker, no sign, no grave even, to indicate the resting place of this powerful queen of the twelfth century. A question to the priest of the group that happens to be using the site for services that day will reveal no knowledge or interest in the queen's resting place. The tomb and sacred space associated with it is a religious place, celebrating the holy, not a place for secular rulers to be acknowledged or noticed. This attitude is a perfect reflection of the attitudes of scores of historians and chroniclers who passed over Queen Melisende's contributions because she did not fit in with the prevailing notions of the time and place.

These attitudes make it all the more remarkable that Queen Melisende was able to rule at all, and especially that she was able to rule as effectively as she did. What would it have been like for Queen Melisende as a ruler in the twelfth century? In some ways, the roles of women were less circumscribed in the twelfth century than they would be in the thirteenth, when the church and secular courts conspired to reduce the rights and privileges of women. Yet consider this description of the role of women from a history of medieval life: 'In every case, women were officially seen as standing in a position of subordination to men, and their powers of choice were always circumscribed to a greater or lesser degree by both official social structures and unofficial customs.'[1]

In some ways, the geographical distance between Jerusalem and Europe, and the special requirements of life in the Crusader states, created a space in which Queen Melisende could function as she did. But still, Queen Melisende had to walk a very narrow line to preserve the respect of the nobles and her subjects as both woman and queen.

As Bernard of Clairvaux cautioned her in the letter quoted in chapter one: 'You must set your hand to great things and, although a woman, you must act as a man by doing all you have to do "in a spirit prudent and strong".' Do great things; be a woman; act like a man—a tall order, but not unlike what is asked of women leaders and politicians in our own day. What can be appreciated today, perhaps even more so than in her own time, is that Queen Melisende was able to actually do those things, and to rule over a fractious kingdom as queen in her own right.

In uncovering the identity of Queen Melisende, one must look at the many factors shaping her life. Some facts we know: her mother was an Armenian princess, her father was a French Crusader. She was born in Edessa, into her mother's family which had lived there for generations. She must have been highly influenced by the Armenian culture of her mother, as those relatives would have been close by during the early years of her life. She was surrounded too by her father's 'family', those Crusaders who were his comrades, many of whom were also his relations.

We also must not ignore or minimize the fact that she had a multicultural background and was raised neither totally in the world from which her mother came, nor totally in the world from which her father came, but a world apart, made up of elements of each. Amin Maalouf refers to this complexity when he describes his own situation as both a Lebanese and a Frenchman: 'What makes me myself rather than anyone else is the very fact that I am poised between two countries, two or three languages, and several cultural traditions. It is precisely this that defines my identity.'[2] The same might be said of Queen Melisende, and I have tried to present aspects of each of the cultures which influenced her in order to more fully understand her and the world in which she lived.

Her life must have been shaped by exposure to constant conflict and the comings and goings of her father. As the eldest child, and having no brothers, she must have realized the importance of her position from an early age, and especially after her father became king. The fact that we have documents signed by both King Baldwin II and Melisende reflects the importance he must have accorded her as well.[3] Considering the difficulty of exposing the true nature of Queen Melisende, I have chosen to tell her story through the art that surely would have filled the public and private spaces of her life.[4]

One of the foremost 'jobs' of the monarch was to commission and promote artistic expression that would enhance the image and position of the ruler. The role of royalty as patrons of the arts is as old as the concept of royalty itself. Rulers used their wealth and power to have works produced which would glorify them in the eyes of their subjects and as a statement of their greatness. Patronage also served political and social aims, as it could be used to buy loyalty as well as serve the common good—the building of religious edifices and hospitals, for example.

For Queen Melisende, the patronage of religious orders and establishments helped consolidate her power by insuring the loyalty of church officials. She was renowned in her own day for her lavish gifts and grants to the religious establishment.[5] Indeed, her reign marked a particularly harmonious period between the ruling powers and the Latin Church. She was especially solicitous of the welfare of the Eastern Orthodox Churches of the region, among them the Syrian Orthodox and the Armenian Church.[6] This was largely due, no doubt, to the fact that her mother was Armenian, but also because she had grown up surrounded by a variety of religious traditions. Her personal interest and support of all the Christian sects in Jerusalem must have endeared her to the people as well as securing the support of the Latin Church.

The period during which Queen Melisende reigned was known to be a time of enthusiastic building activity. The desire to consolidate and reinforce the idea of the Crusader state took form in building and/or remaking existing buildings to reflect the Crusader presence.

One of the religious structures that benefited especially from the largesse and patronage of Queen Melisende is the Church of St Anne, rebuilt in the 1140s (and much restored by the French in 1800s). Melisende's sister, Yvetta, was a nun in the cloisters associated with this site. There had originally been a Byzantine church commemorating two events: the Healing of the Paralytic (John 5), and the birth of the Virgin Mary at the home of her parents, Anne and Joachim. The Crusaders separated the sites of these two events, building a larger, basilica-type church to honour the place of the birth of the Virgin, and a smaller structure on the original site to signify the location of the Healing of the Paralytic.[7] The church illustrates how the three cultural traditions of the area combine in one building: early Christian and Muslim influences are seen in the aisled basilica and dome in front of the central apse; the Byzantine element is evidenced by the use of the dome; and the Romanesque tradition of Europe in areas of decoration and structure.[8]

Arguably the most important building project undertaken by Queen Melisende when she ruled with her husband Fulk was the remodelling of the Church of the Holy Sepulchre. The structure had been associated with the burial of Christ and His resurrection since Emperor Constantine the Great ordered a church built on the site in 326-333.[9] The church was largely destroyed by the Fatimid caliph al-Hakim in 1009, but the site remained a place of pilgrimage and the church was rebuilt using its original foundations by the Byzantine emperor, Constantine Monomachus, in 1048.

If Jerusalem was the centre of the world to Europeans, the Church of the Holy Sepulchre was its very navel. The importance of the church as a primary place of pilgrimage as well as its use in crowning the rulers of the kingdom and installing the patriarchs dictated the form it took as it was re-designed by the Crusaders.[10] Not only was it necessary to make the interior more spacious and user-friendly, but the Crusaders needed to stamp this holy site with their own imprint, as a statement of their power and control over Jerusalem.

The connection between Queen Melisende and the rebuilding of the Church is well documented, and she had exceptional power during these years.[11] We can assume she worked closely with the patriarch in making decisions about the building campaign. It was a tremendous and important undertaking. Every aspect of the rebuilding reflected

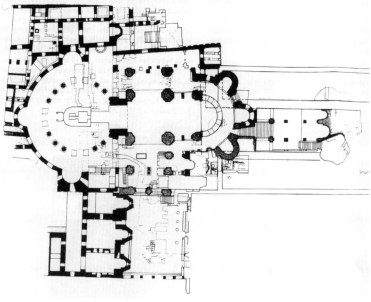

5.1 Plan of the Church of the Holy Sepulchre

back on the Crusader state and especially the monarchs who planned and participated in it. William of Tyre describes it thus: 'they enlarged the original church and added to it a new building of massive and lofty construction, which enclosed the old church and in marvellous wise included within its precincts the holy places.'[12]

The challenge of incorporating existing structures into a new design must have been significant (see pl. 5.1). To enclose the open courtyard of the previous structure, the Crusaders built a basilica with a nave and four aisles, a transept with a dome where it intersects the nave, and an ambulatory with three chapels radiating from it. This new structure created a balance with the existing Rotunda, with its three apses, to the west. At the south-eastern corner of the basilica, a chapel was added to mark the site of the Crucifixion.

The entrance to the church as a whole was, and still is, a double portal leading into the transept (pl. 5.2). This portal originally

5.2 South transept entrance to the Church of the Holy Sepulchre, Jerusalem, 1149.

had mosaics decorating the tympanum (now lost). There is still doubt about what exactly the mosaics depicted.[13] In European medieval churches, a scene of the Last Judgement, or Christ in Majesty would have been depicted in relief sculpture on the tympanum. But here the decoration, being in mosaic, would have reflected the Byzantine influence. As such, it also appropriated the power and wealth of that empire, and added to the status of this most holy site. The significance of this would not have been lost on those entering through this portal.

The lintels over the doors (arguably dated from about 1150) also convey important messages about the significance of the church and its importance to the Crusaders who reclaimed it. The lintels are very damaged, and no longer *in situ*, but they are still on view at the Rockefeller Museum in Jerusalem (pls 5.3 and 5.4).

The scenes on the western lintel have been the subject of much scholarly debate, including the identification of some of the scenes themselves. The scenes are divided into five distinct panels by the use of architectural elements in the background of the scenes.

One scholar identifies the scenes, from left to right, as: the Raising of Lazarus; the Imploring of Christ by Mary and Martha; Christ Giving Instruction for the preparation of the Last Supper; the Entry into Jerusalem; and the Last Supper. While there are problems in reading the scenes from left to right because they are not in proper chronological order, the order of the scenes relates to the sequence

5.3 *Church of the Holy Sepulchre, western lintel, The Last Supper.*

5.4 *Western lintel, Raising of Lazarus.*

of sites a twelfth-century pilgrim would have visited and follows the liturgical procession of Palm Sunday.[14]

Another scholar, N Kedar, offers a different reading of the identity of the scenes, and starts the interpretation of the scenes with the larger central scene, which is identified as the Expulsion of the Merchants and Cleansing of the Temple. Christ is standing higher in the cleansed temple while three groups of people represent unbelievers and their rejected sacrifices.[15] This is not the traditional version of this story, but it fits in with the concept that the Crusaders' foremost aim in conquering Jerusalem was to remove the infidels and establish the Latin Kingdom. This link is strengthened by the fact that the taking of Jerusalem on 15 July and the consecration of the Church of the Holy Sepulchre were celebrated annually on the same day.

The other panels are described by Mr Kedar as being pendants to the central panel. The Triumphal Entry of Christ into Jerusalem to the right would have been especially meaningful to the Crusaders as a symbol of their own triumphal entry. The scene to the left of the centre is traditionally read as the Imploring of Christ by Mary and

Martha. Kedar redefines this scene as the Apparition of Christ after the Resurrection, with the two kneeling women Martha and Mary in the Garden, the three men on Christ's right as pilgrims, and the four on His left as apostles.

The outer scenes are undisputed as the Raising of Lazarus on the extreme left, and the Last Supper on the extreme right. The Raising of Lazarus is traditionally interpreted as Christ's triumph over death, and the Last Supper as the promise of eternal life.

The reading of the lintel according to Kedar offers an interpretation that reinforces the Crusaders mission and accomplishment of cleansing the temple and establishing the kingdom, one which would have been obvious and appreciated by the Crusaders and pilgrims entering through that door into the place of death and resurrection of Christ.[16] However, either reading of the images on this lintel leads to a connection to the interior sites of Christ's death and resurrection.

The lintel above the eastern portal of the entrance complements the western lintel in its message of Christ's crucifixion as a path of salvation (pls 5.5 and 5.6). We have already seen the vine scroll motif in the ivory covers of the Queen Melisende Psalter and again on the back of the Denkendorf reliquary (see pl. 5.15). Here we see the same motif used in yet a different way and in a different medium. The men, centaur, siren, and birds entwined in the vine scroll symbolize man caught in a web of sin, the path out of which is shown by Christ's sacrifice—the story on the western lintel.[17]

The decoration of the lintel is arranged in five large medallions evenly spaced along the centre of the lintel, and separated by pairs of smaller medallions, one above the other. The medallions form part of a continuous vine scroll wound around a central bough. This is thought to refer to the transformation of the Cross of Christ and His suffering into the Tree of Life.[18] This seems an appropriate symbol to use above a door leading to the scene of Christ's death and resurrection. Even here we find a hidden reference to the expulsion of the infidel from Jerusalem, for the stone used for this lintel was re-used, and the reverse side has a Fatimid sculpture relief (pl. 5.7).

One scholar suggests that the tympanum above each door would have been decorated with mosaics appropriate to the holy sites of Jerusalem, and perhaps including the Crucifixion. If this is true, we can see that the decoration of the portals would have been much more striking and unified iconographically.[19]

5.5 Eastern lintel, detail.

In the end, the architects and builders who remodelled the Church of the Holy Sepulchre seem to have created a finished product that fulfilled the needs of pilgrim and Crusader.[20] They entered through doors above which were depicted scenes of power and pilgrimage; as they entered the church itself, the worshippers had a view of all the important areas

5.6 Eastern lintel, detail.

5.7 Back of eastern lintel, Fatimid sculpture.

in the interior, the main altar, the altars in the radial chapels, and the site of the Crucifixion and the Resurrection.[21]

The design itself would have been recognizable to visitors and pilgrims from the West, as it has elements of the pilgrimage churches there, such as the ambulatory and the three radiating chapels around the apse. There are Byzantine features as well, such as the south façade with its double portal and mosaic decoration.[22] For Queen Melisende and others from the surrounding region, the clearly eastern feature of the dome which adds a vertical orientation to the inside of the Church, would have been comforting and familiar.[23] Colour plate 5.8 and plates 5.9 through 5.12 show views and details from the Church of the Holy Sepulchre.

The scriptorium of the Church of the Holy Sepulchre also produced works that reflect the rich variety of artistic styles coming together in Jerusalem under Queen Melisende's reign. These included the illuminated pages of the Queen Melisende Psalter. The manuscript of the psalter contains twenty-four full-page New Testament illuminations; a calendar with twelve zodiac-sign medallions; eight full-page initials in gold ground with *incipits* in gold for the liturgical divisions of the psalms; a complete text of psalter decorations with gold initials; and nine portraits of the saints in headpiece panels.[24]

The example in colour plate 5.13 copies the Byzantine tradition of depicting Christ enthroned with the Virgin Mary on his left and St John the Baptist on his right. This scene was called the *Deesis*. In Greek the word means 'entreaty'. The concept is that the Virgin Mary and John the Baptist will interact with Christ on the viewer's (supplicant's) behalf. It commonly appeared as a full-page miniature in Byzantine psalter manuscripts. The Byzantine model is apparent in every way. The figures of the Virgin Mary and St John are elongated, with static and traditional gestures. Christ is enthroned, holding a book and giving the sign of blessing. The figures are flat and two-dimensional. Even the colour and style of the drapery follow Byzantine formulae. The entire page evokes the glory of Byzantium and would have been meant to confer upon this manuscript the same.

The person believed to have been the artist of all the New Testament miniatures in the psalter is Basilius, whose name appears incised on the ground of the footstool of this page. The name is Greek, but the use of the Latin form for his name was common, even by Westerners in the Holy Land. There is scholarly debate on where the artist might have come from. Perhaps he had his early training

5.9 *Church of the Holy Sepulchre, capitals of transept façade.*

5.10 *Church of the Holy Sepulchre, moulding of transept façade.*

5.11 *Church of the Holy Sepulchre, view to main portal.*

5.12 *Church of the Holy Sepulchre, view to choir vault and apse from dome.*

in the West and studied in Constantinople, afterwards coming to work in Jerusalem for the royal court.[25] Or perhaps he was born in the East and absorbed elements of Byzantine, Western, and Eastern art.[26] The very fact that his origins are disputed by scholars shows the likely probability that artists working in Jerusalem were studying and certainly exposed to the rich traditions that met in Jerusalem during Queen Melisende's time.

It is easy to see how different the image of the Archangel Michael in colour plate 3.1 is from the previous image. They are both from the Queen Melisende Psalter. Again we see Byzantine elements in the flattening of the figure and the costume of the angel. The colours in his garment are reflected in the border of the image. The style of clothing and its reflection of Byzantine imperial dress have been discussed in chapter three. It is significant that St Michael, the avenging angel of God, should be displayed prominently in a book celebrating the military and diplomatic successes of the Crusader kingdom.

In another example from the Queen Melisende Psalter we see yet another style, and probably a different artist. This full page letter B (from *Beatus Vir*) marks the beginning of a chapter (col. pl. 5.14). This is called the *incipit* page, and it was common in both Western and Byzantine art to have such a page as a decorative marker of a new chapter. The appearance of King David in the lower bowl of the 'B' indicates this as the beginning of a psalm.

The page is covered with gold leaf, and the letter outlined in black. The intricacy of the decoration evokes both Western Anglo-Saxon decoration and Islamic design elements. The form of the letter and inhabited scroll design is similar to manuscript art found in northern Europe, especially England.[27] One can appreciate the imagination of the artist in the variety of animals and mythical beings entwined in the foliage. In the upright column of the letter is a dragon-like creature and a centaur with bow and arrow. Above the mask joining the two bowls of the 'B' is a leonine creature with a beaked bird head. Above it on the left is a bird, and on the right a siren. Disguised but not invisible, these inhabitants invite close scrutiny. The visual complexity creates a delightful and rewarding viewing experience. Other pages contain initials illustrating similar design elements.

In addition to patronage of architectural projects and work from the scriptorium at the Church of the Holy Sepulchre, Queen Melisende would have been instrumental in commissioning decorative arts of all kinds. These would have included reliquaries to hold holy relics for use as gifts to visitors of high rank; portable objects made from ivory or metalwork; and large works of iron or stone to adorn buildings.

The one item with the highest value for a visiting religious personage would have been a piece of the True Cross. The legend of the finding of the True Cross involves Helena, the mother of Constantine I. She is said to have gone on pilgrimage to Jerusalem to find the cross on which Christ was crucified. She achieved this by calling together the Jews and asking the whereabouts of the True Cross. They lead her to three crosses, and the 'True' Cross was determined when it miraculously brought a dead man back to life. She left part of the Cross in Jerusalem, and brought part of it back to Constantine in Constantinople.[28] Pieces of it were thereafter distributed as a sign of great honour.

An object believed to have had so much contact with the holy body of Christ was bound to be imbued with His holy spirit. Christians venerated the True Cross, and believed it contained special healing powers. Reliquaries were made to house the sliver of the True Cross and bestowed upon the deserving person by leaders of the Church and the king[29] (presumably the queen had this privilege as well). These reliquaries, containing as they did an object of such inestimable value, were made of the finest materials with the best craftsmanship available. In Jerusalem during Queen Melisende's time, the workshops of goldworkers were set up along a street close to the Church of the Holy Sepulchre for just this purpose.[30]

The reliquary in plate 5.15 was given by the Patriarch of Jerusalem to a pilgrim from the monastery of the Holy Sepulchre in Denkendorf Germany. This reliquary gives us an idea of the meeting of different

5.15 Reliquary of the True Cross from Denkendorf, front and back, Jerusalem, c. 1130. (Photos: P Frankenstein, H Zwietasch; Landesmuseum Württemberg, Stuttgart)

artistic traditions that was so prevalent in Jerusalem during Queen Melisende's reign. This example has both Western and Byzantine styles. It is thought that the goldsmiths in Jerusalem came from Europe. Once there, they studied Byzantine designs and craftsmanship, thus would have been adept in combining the two traditions.[31]

The cross is made of silver and covered with gold. Its shape is different from the single-armed, or Latin cross, and also from the orthodox, or Byzantine cross, which has two cross arms as here but an additional, smaller crossbar called a *supedaneum* at an angle below. This cross reflects the shape that was associated with the True Cross. The slits in the front of the cross reveal the piece of the True Cross beneath. The six quatrefoils at the ends of the slit openings contained small stones of the Holy Sepulchre mounted in the centres. This type of double reliquary would have been appropriate for its destination, which was a church named after the Church of the Holy Sepulchre in

Denkendorf. The semi-precious stones on the front, along with pearls and amethysts, are set in pairs around the quatrefoils and along the slit opening. This kind of filigree decoration, the stamped impressions, and the quatrefoil designs come from the Byzantine tradition. The medallion with the Lamb of God in the centre and the medallions of saints at the extremities of the cross on the reverse side is Western in origin.[32]

This cross and other types of reliquaries for pieces of the True Cross would have been important export items to Europe. In addition to their religious function and beauty of craftsmanship, they would have been reminders of the importance of the Crusades and a possible incentive for others to 'take the Cross'. They also served to expose Western patrons and craftsmen to the artistic legacy of the Eastern world.

In addition to Queen Melisende's religious patronage and the religious objects associated with the holy sites in Jerusalem, she would have gone to great lengths, like all rulers of the time, to ensure that her visitors would be impressed with the decoration and objects in her private apartments, as well as the public spaces where she held court. In the self-conscious atmosphere of a royal setting, competition with Byzantium, the Islamic courts, and the courts of Europe would have been a factor. We know that Muslim and Crusader rulers exchanged luxury gifts as part of political life.[33] These items would have been found in homes of the wealthy and at court. They were easily portable and could also have been taken back to Europe, where they would have been prized as much for their exotic value as for the material out of which they were made and their richness of decoration. In the end, however, the use of these objects by the royal court was not only because of the status they could convey, but also simply because they were beautiful.

Trade was flourishing in the twelfth century. In spite of the fighting between the Crusaders and Muslims, caravans still crossed the desert, the Italian merchant ships still sailed from Crusader ports, and luxury goods from Byzantium, Iran, and Egypt still found their way into the courts of the Middle East and Europe.[34] The competition between

131

the courts for these goods was lively, and gifts of luxury objects were often exchanged. These gifts served the purpose of flattering and bribing the recipients, as well as impressing them with the wealth and taste of the bestower.

It must be remembered that those Crusaders who decided to stay, as newly arrived inhabitants of the kingdom of Jerusalem after the First Crusade, would, by necessity as well as by inclination, have needed to adapt their lifestyles to the requirements of the climate and customs of their new home. The newcomers soon learned that the winters, while severe, were also short. The summers, by contrast, were long and hot. In order to adjust to these realities, they had also to adjust their habits of dress, food, and lifestyle.[35] For the First Crusaders, this must have been quite an adjustment indeed, but for Queen Melisende and the children of other Frankish nobility, these factors would have been accepted as an integral part of their lives. Especially for Queen Melisende, whose mother was also a native of the region, the way of life adopted by the First Crusaders would have seemed completely natural and comfortable.

Since the majority of Westerners left after the capture of Jerusalem, the Franks made up a distinct minority of the total population of the region. They would have been surrounded by native Christians and Muslims of the area. Their servants and those with whom they had any business would have been from these groups. To understand and cope with unfamiliar territory, climate, health, and customs, they would have needed at first to rely on the local population.[36]

The constant contact with their Muslim neighbours, and the mutual dependency on trade between the two groups ensured that objects of everyday life as well as luxury items would find their way into every Frankish household. The lifestyle of the Franks in Queen Melisende's time was in stark contrast to life in Europe, and this was remarked upon by those who came later.

The fact of life in Outremer (literally, from the French, 'beyond the sea', and a word used to denote the Crusader states) and the Crusaders accommodation with it, was a shock to those who came from Europe after the First Crusade, as reinforcements for the Crusaders, or as pilgrims. One chronicler of the Crusades, Fulcher of Chartres, commented on this fact:

> … Consider, I pray, and reflect how in our time God has transferred the West into the East. For we who were Occidentals now have been made Orientals … We have already forgotten the places of our birth; they have become unknown to many of us, or, at least, are unmentioned.[37]

Later, a European visitor, James of Vitry, expressed the dismay and even contempt that some felt toward the children of the first generation of Crusaders: 'They were brought up in luxury, soft and effeminate, more used to baths than battles, addicted to unclean and riotous living, clad like women in soft robes.'[38]

In 1128, the royal residence was moved from its former location in the Aqsa Mosque to the Citadel.[39] When we imagine the interior of the royal palace in Jerusalem, we can safely assume that there were windows with glass panes which were manufactured in the area and in common use. There would have been mosaic decoration on the walls and floors, as the best artisans of this craft were the Byzantines and Muslims who were either resident, or brought in for the task. The furniture would have been of the highest quality, with carved decoration on the legs of the tables and chairs. Silk cushions would have made the seats more comfortable. We can also imagine a writing table, perhaps inlaid with various woods or mother-of-pearl.[40]

At dinner time there certainly would have been a table covered with the finest damask cloth woven nearby in Damascus. Gold and silver serving items with elaborate decoration would have been conspicuously on view. Likewise there would have been silver eating and serving utensils. Glass beakers and lustreware bowls would have been used. As Steven Runciman says: 'There were carpets and damask hangings, elegantly carved and inlaid tables and coffers …, dinner-services in gold and silver, cutlery, fine faience and even a few dishes of porcelain from the Farther East.'[41]

Flavourful, spiced dishes of food like that described in Chapter 4 would have been served. The guests, who must have included both orientalized Christians and visitors or pilgrims from Europe, would have been dressed either in the light, beautifully patterned silks from the East, or the rugged and much coarser fabric from the West.

We can imagine the public and private spaces of Queen Melisende's household filled with the sumptuous art available in the region, and imported from elsewhere: lustreware ceramics from Egypt; gold, silver, and inlaid vessels for use at the table and in the private apartments; buckets for liquid soap used in the bath; rosewater sprinklers; inkstands from Iran; engraved glass from Syria and Egypt. Based on archaeological evidence of glass beakers and glazed pottery found at Crusader sites, we can surmise that all of the wealthier classes of Crusaders had developed a taste for luxury goods of the Middle East.[42] Items from the West could scarcely compete with the variety and quality of goods available on Queen Melisende's doorstep.

Dishes like the one in colour plate 5.16 would have been prominently displayed and must have impressed visitors to the court. This is an earthenware bowl covered with an opaque white glaze and painted in copper red lustre. It follows the twelfth-century Egyptian practice of using lustre for the background and details, with the main features left in white.[43] The result is striking, as the figure of the lion and hare stand out against the shimmery gold of the background. This bowl was surely meant to compete with metalwork and imitate the effects of gold. The technique allows the artist greater freedom to portray the lion as strolling (or stalking) through flowers or leaves, while the hare leaps across his back. This expression of movement and naturalism was in keeping with the artistic trends of the time. Featuring animals as a central theme was common in all media, as we have seen.

The sides of the bowl contain an untranslated kufic inscription, surrounded by spiralling scrolls. The angular script lends a pleasing symmetry to the piece and creates a frame for the central image. The appearance of the script gives the object a blessing that would have been imparted to the person who used it.

Likewise the gold wine bowl from west Iran, dated to the eleventh century (col. pl. 5.17). The image of the ducks and the decorative medallion on the side of the bowl are similar to the patterns in textiles of the time. The writing along the rim can be traced to a tenth-century poem by Ibn al-Tammar, and identify the bowl's use for wine. The text says:

> Wine is a sun in a garment of red Chinese silk.
> It flows; its source is the flask.
> Drink, then, in the pleasance of time, since our day
> Is a day of delight which has brought dew.[44]

Even though objects such as these contained Arabic script and came from a land against which the Crusaders fought, they would have been valued for their beauty and craftsmanship and used with pride by their Western owner. In some cases, use of these objects affirmed the conquest of the people who created them, and so were also symbols of the power of the conqueror.

The size and shape of the glass perfume sprinkler (col. pl. 5.18) would have made it easy to handle. The decorative trailed design on the neck of the sprinkler gives it a distinctive character. One can imagine Queen Melisende using such an item to perfume her hair and clothes, as did men and women of all ranks.

We can also imagine Queen Melisende using other glass objects of exquisite beauty on an everyday basis. This tiny glass bowl (col. pl. 5.19), 7.7 cm. high and 11.2 cm. in diameter, from Egypt, made in the eleventh or twelfth century, is a case in point. Tiny though it is, its slightly swelling shape with its fifteen vertical ribs and stained decoration lend a delicacy and grace that is striking.[45]

Likewise we can imagine the queen and courtiers drinking from glass beakers such as the one in colour plate 5.20. This style of beaker was made in Syria in the twelfth to thirteenth century and was widely exported over the region.[46] They would have been relatively inexpensive, thus accessible even for those not of the wealthy class.

There were also glass objects of the much more precious material of rock crystal. Perhaps these would have been better suited to the table of a queen. These rare objects were considered as valuable as gold or silver objects.[47] They were valued not only for their beauty, but also because they were so difficult to carve. A solid piece of rock crystal had to be hollowed out by hand to the desired thickness. The outer surface was then carefully carved.[48] There are examples of ewers and phials, and also, as shown here in plate 5.21, chess pieces. Thus these luxurious objects would have graced dressing, dining, and game tables of the queen. In Europe, we find the best examples of rock crystal in church treasuries. Because of the precious nature of the material, it was used in making reliquaries or for liturgical vessels. Objects of rock crystal from Islamic lands may also have been appropriated for church use.

Beautiful glass containers (col. pl. 5.22) were used to hold eye makeup. Though the glass in this example looks almost black, it is actually a deep blue. The white design is made by applying opaque white molten glass, then rolling the vessel on a stone surface. This technique is called marvering, and was widely used for vessels of this type. The flask was not meant to stand upright, but to be placed at an angle on some kind of support. Its small size (typically 12-15 cm. in height) was well suited for holding the black *kohl*, or eye makeup, which was applied to the eyelid with a metal applicator.[49]

Queen Melisende's clothes must have been made from the wide variety of cloth so expertly woven in the region. These included silk, brocade, wool, and finely woven muslin.[50] Again, from Steven Runciman: 'The ladies adopted the traditional eastern fashion of a long under-robe, and a short tunic or coat, heavily embroidered with gold thread and maybe with jewels. In winter they wore furs, as did their husbands. Out of doors they were veiled like the Muslim women, but less generously covered with paint; and they affected a mincing gait.

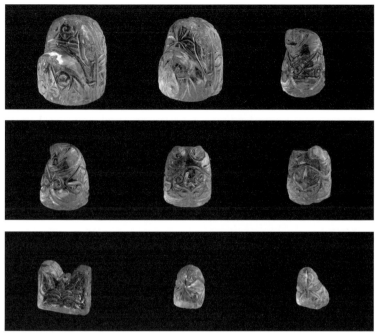

5.21 Carved rock crystal chess pieces, Fatimid, late 9th-10 century, probably Egypt.
(© The al-Sabah Collection, Dar al-Athar al-Islamiyyah, Kuwait)

But, for all their airs of delicacy and languor, they were as courageous as their husbands and brothers. Many a noblewoman was called upon to lead the defence of her castle in the absence of her lord.'[51]

Because of the fragile nature of textiles, we have few examples of the style and patterns of the time. Most of what we do have is preserved because it was used to wrap relics which were sent back to Europe and stored in church treasuries. We can also get a sense of the beautiful patterns from manuscripts of the time. We can be sure that Queen Melisende did her best to compete with the Byzantine court in manners of dress.

Few examples of fabrics from the time of Queen Melisende survive. Weaving techniques in the region were highly developed, and materials of silk, linen and cotton were readily available. Often the fabrics depicted lions and eagles which, while primarily decorative, were meant to symbolize power as well.[52] The fact that the example in colour plate 5.23 contains kufic inscriptions does not preclude it from being worn by Queen Melisende or other members of the court. They would have appreciated the quality of the silk cloth and the bright and colourful designs. While this fragment gives us an idea of what material would have been available, fabrics were also embellished with pearls, gold ornaments, and precious gems. It is certain that that Queen Melisende exploited the possibilities of dress in presenting a visual image of herself reflecting her station as Queen of the Kingdom of Jerusalem. As such, her clothes would have been made from the finest fabrics available.

With these few examples, we can get only the mere hint of the scope and quality of objects available to Queen Melisende. So much of the metalwork was melted down, so much of the glass and pottery destroyed. But the examples we do have show us the marked contrast between life in the Eastern Mediterranean during the twelfth century, and that of Europe during the same years. After the First Crusade, objects like these made their way into Europe in increasing numbers. After the sack of Constantinople during the Fourth Crusade, the trickle of objects became a flood. The artistic styles and techniques of the East influenced art in the West. It was not just the meeting of artistic traditions that influenced this transformation, but the opening of the European mind as increasing numbers of Crusaders and pilgrims encountered the rich and sophisticated cultures of Byzantium and Islam. This fortunate confluence of circumstances had lasting impact on both the culture and art of the West.

6

BEYOND THE COURT OF QUEEN MELISENDE

Not long after Queen Melisende's death in 1161, her own son, Baldwin III, died. Thereafter the kingdom was torn apart by internal power struggles, fragmenting the fighting forces and allowing the waiting Muslim armies to gain the upper hand. The great Muslim leader Saladin captured Jerusalem in 1187 and it was once again in Muslim hands.

For the next hundred years, in spite of further intervention by European reinforcements, both large and small, the Crusader holdings dwindled. Little by little, even these last strongholds were lost. Finally, in 1291, Acre, the last bastion of Crusader presence, was abandoned and the era of the Crusades to the Holy Land was over.[1]

During Melisende's reign, the Crusader states had coalesced into something resembling a cohesive entity. Though the coalition was always fragile, Queen Melisende contributed to the dynastic stability of the kingdom because she was the daughter of a king, the wife of a king, the mother of a king, and ruled, in the absence of the men in her life, as queen in her own right. Indeed, her reign spans a time period when all the factors were ripe for creating a 'golden age' for artistic production. It was a time of consolidation of power (as much as this ever took place among the fighting nobles of the kingdom) and territory, and a need for artistic statements of power and hegemony. As we have seen in the Queen Melisende Psalter and the lintels of the Church of the Holy Sepulchre, there was an attempt to link artistic expression of the aim of the Crusaders—the establishment of the Crusader kingdom—to Old and New Testament imagery.

The art produced in Jerusalem during Melisende's reign helped to inform and transform the art of Europe in subsequent centuries.

This is not to say that Crusader art of the period was the only factor in that transformation. This is the subject of much debate in scholarly circles. It is even difficult to say what, exactly, Crusader art is. Perhaps Jaroslav Folda comes closest with this statement:

> Crusader art was the response of Frankish patrons and their artists to the orientalism and Christian multiculturalism of the Latin East, exciting creative ideas of style and iconography, meaning and content, which were integrated with the Western traditions that were their heritage, directly or indirectly, to produce a distinctive and original result.[2]

By this definition we can see how closely Queen Melisende and the years of her rule are connected with the elements that Folda describes as Crusader art.

From 1187 on, Jerusalem ceased to be the centre for rulers of the Crusaders. This meant it could also no longer be the centre of artistic production. The years spanning Queen Melisende's reign figure prominently as the time when the Crusader state was most solid and cohesive. During that time, Jerusalem was the centre for art production that reflected the aims and aspirations of the Crusaders. Thirty years before her reign, the Crusaders states were just being born; thirty years after her reign they were in decline and Jerusalem was back in Muslim hands.

The presence of a powerful queen presiding over a relatively stable kingdom provided an environment in which the artisans from many different traditions could come together in one place to share and produce an art in which there was much cross pollination of techniques, styles, and ideas. This fact, together with the many building campaigns taking place during her reign, places Melisende in the centre of this rich cultural milieu.

It is often difficult to untangle the strands of artistic influence. Europe, the Byzantine Empire, and much of the Muslim world had a shared Graeco-Roman heritage. Likewise artistic motifs from Persia found their way into both Byzantine and Islamic art. The art and culture of the Byzantine Empire had a significant impact on European art, and a section of this chapter is devoted to illustrate that. But it was the Crusades that enhanced and hastened the effect of all these artistic motifs and techniques in Europe. Examples of Eastern craftsmanship and artistry in all media made their way there after the First Crusade. This profoundly influenced artistic production there, and there are profuse examples of the enduring nature of the influence in the art of the period of the Crusades and after. The art in the court of Queen Melisende provided a model for integrating and combining the cultural strands of East and West.

Economics played a prominent role, and it might be said that the Crusades cracked open the nut of Eastern commerce for Europe. Prior to the twelfth century, the port cities of Italy were the entry points for goods which came from Byzantium and the Islamic world. The international trade routes which crossed the interiors of these empires were off limits for Europeans, and were jealously guarded by the governments of the lands through which they passed. This assured that those governments reaped the benefits of such commerce: taxes and customs duties.[3]

These restrictions broke down when the Crusaders captured towns and territory that allowed merchants from Europe to penetrate into the commercial centres of the Middle East itself. William of Tyre writes about one such city, Alexandria:

> Alexandria has the reputation of receiving a larger supply of wares of every description than any other maritime city. Whatever our world lacks in spices, pearls, oriental treasures and foreign wares is brought hither from the two Indies, Saba, Arabia, even from both the Ethiopias and from Persia and other lands nearby. Thus masses of people from East and West flock thither, making Alexandria the public mart of both worlds.[4]

Primary among the sought-after products of these markets were cloth and spices. When a medieval merchant speaks of spices, he is including the seasonings we usually associate with the word, but also perfumes, incense, dyes and related products, condiments of all kinds, and medicines.[5]

Textiles were produced in Europe in Flanders and northern Italy, but they could not compare with the quality of products coming from the East. The vibrant colours and exotic materials of Eastern workmanship made them one of the most sought after symbols of wealth, taste, and prestige. Indeed, even the names of materials evoke their place of manufacture: damask from Damascus; satin from Zayton in China.[6] Baldacco was the Italian name for Baghdad, and from it, the term *baldacchino* is used to designate luxury cloth, particularly that used for canopies.[7]

Fine silks such as those shown in colour plates 3.11, 4.14, and 5.23 found their way to the West. Because of the value and status associated with them, many of these materials were made into ecclesiastical garments. When they became worn, pieces were often used to wrap relics, or sometimes textile fragments arrived in the west because they protected relics coming from the East. Because of that, many of these pieces of material were preserved in church treasuries.[8]

The same designs were used in different media and Western workshops often adopted Middle Eastern motifs for decorative objects. The object pictured in colour plate 6.1, which is a pitcher, or ewer, is an example. We can see how the artisans of Mosan (in present-day Belgium) have adapted the shape from eastern representations in silks like the one referenced above. Ewers during the twelfth century often took the form of real or fantastical animals.

Bathing was very common in the Middle East, both domestically and for religious purposes, and decorative objects for this purpose were common. Even though washing was not as common in Europe in the twelfth century, these containers were created out of ceramics or precious metals. Often called *aquamanilia* (from the Latin for water—*aqua*, and hand—*manus*), these decorative and sometimes whimsical ewers were used for washing at home, but especially at church, where the ritual washing of hands before Mass and in other Christian rites such as baptism was important. The ewer was meant to be filled through the opening in the tail, which had a lid (now missing); the mouth of the beast is the spout.

6.2 Lion aquamanile, 1200-1250, German, Lower Saxony.

The decorating of a base metal with inlay was a common way of elevating the status and value of an object in the Middle East. The same techniques are employed here: silver for highlighting the breast wing, and tail detail of the ewer; niello for decoration on the front wing and to emphasize the facial features and silver inlay.

We can see here some of the ways that Islamic forms and decorative techniques were adopted and adapted by the Christian West. The metalworkers of the Mosan region needed no lessons in fine craftsmanship from the Muslims, but it is clear they were open to ideas that came with returning Crusaders and the Eastern goods they brought with them.

Besides the Mosan region, Lower Saxony was the other major production area for bronze cast *aquamanilia*. Animal-shaped *aquamanilia* continued to be made and used in these two areas, both for domestic and ecclesiastical patrons (pl. 6.2). They followed the style and mechanics of *aquamanilia* from Islamic lands in that they had an opening in the head to put in the water, and a spout coming out the mouth of the animal.[9] The lion was an especially popular shape, both because of the animal itself and its connotations of strength and power. To have such an object on the table would have given status to any medieval patron. Their widespread use can be attested by the fact that there are more than 350 such objects known that were made between the twelfth and fifteenth centuries.[10]

Even some of the more humble decorative arts from Islamic lands found their way to the West and were absorbed into the local culture. The Islamic ceramics were a colourful and visually stimulating contrast to the rather mundane and drab ceramics of Europe. In Italy, pottery bowls with Islamic designs could be found used as decoration on the exterior of buildings. These bowls were called *bacini,* the Italian word for bowl or basin. They were used as a cheaper alternative to the more expensive mosaic decoration. It did not seem at all unsuitable to use these *bacini* even to decorate churches. The Cathedral of San Miniato near Pisa proudly displayed them on the façade of the church.[11]

Italian potters in later centuries used the superior Islamic ceramics as models, both for design and technique.[12] They were especially influenced by Islamic glazing techniques. Lustre-painting allowed the potters to produce the luminous effect of metal wares. Tin glazes provided the white background on which designs of colour could be applied. Pots with *sgrafitto* design were produced by covering a pot with clay slip, incising a design, and then applying a lead glaze over the whole.[13] The influence of these techniques stimulated technological advances in ceramics in Italy. It is difficult to imagine the subsequent development of Maiolica in Italy without these Islamic precedents.[14]

Many works from the Byzantine world entered Europe through their role as diplomatic gifts. The high esteem in which the Byzantine Empire was held as a centre of learning and sophistication gave its art prestige. As we have seen in illustrations from the Queen Melisende Psalter, by imitating the art, this prestige was transmitted to the artist and the patron.

The miniature in colour plate 6.3 is from an illuminated manuscript made in Constantinople in 1133 and shows the typical Byzantine style of representing a saint. The figure of St Luke is set off by the brilliant gold background. His robes are highlighted and richly patterned.

The miniature in colour plate 6.4, also from a psalter, was made in Würzburg about 1240. It shows the scene of the annunciation. Like the first miniature, the figures are set off against a gold ground. The drapery of the angel is in the same style as the Byzantine model. The style of the Virgin's dress—a veil that covers the head and shoulders and has a star, or cross, on the forehead—copies Byzantine costume.

In yet a third example from a later date (col. pl. 6.5), the same setting of the figure against a gold background is employed. A three quarter portrait rather than a standing figure, it nevertheless bears a resemblance to the Byzantine portrait in the shape of the face and otherworldly quality of the representation. This is a panel painting executed by Simone Martini in the 1330s.

These three examples show the enduring influence of Byzantine religious art on the art of the West. While this influence may have existed regardless of the Crusades or their aftermath, one seminal event brought Byzantine art into Europe in unprecedented quantity. This was the sack of Constantinople in 1204. This act was perpetrated by members of the Fourth Crusade, who had been diverted from their destination of Jerusalem. This occurred when the Crusaders set off from Venice, but did not have the money to pay for their passage from the Venetians. So they plundered Zara, a Christian city on the Dalmatian coast, in order to get the money they needed to pay the Venetians. While there, they encountered a Byzantine prince who had designs on the rulership of Byzantium.

He offered to pay them to install him on the throne. The promise of this payment caused them to divert their course once again, this time to Constantinople. When the prince could not pay them the agreed upon amount, they laid siege to the great city and plundered its riches.[15] In this they were encouraged by the Venetians, who had much to gain from the endeavour. Indeed, the Venetians commercial interests benefited the most from the debacle, as they gained control over territory and trading ports.

An eyewitness account by Gunter of Pairis, Germany, recalls the event: 'So great a wealth of gold and silver, so great a magnificence of

6.6 Bronze horses of San Marco, Venice.

gems and clothing, so great a profusion of valuable trade goods, so great a bounty of foodstuffs, homes so exceptional and so filled with commodities of every sort ... suddenly transformed [the crusaders] from aliens and paupers into very rich citizens.' [16]

The great quantity and quality of riches which made their way into Europe (especially Italy and France) from Constantinople had a lasting effect on artistic production there. Many of the religious items looted became part of the treasuries of Western churches. The Church of San Marco in Venice was a particular recipient of looted goods. This was largely because of the large and influential Venetian merchant colony which already existed in Constantinople, and also because of the Venetian origin of the ships which brought the Fourth Crusaders to the city.

Items such as icons, enamels, reliquaries, relief carvings, and even the four bronze horses (pl. 6.6) taken from the Hippodrome in Constantinople can now be found in Venice.[17]

San Marco itself had been built in imitation of the great churches of Byzantium, specifically the church of the Holy Apostles in

146

Constantinople. The domes and mosaic decoration (col. pl. 6.7) reflect the Byzantine influence. Now they could fill their treasury with original and exquisite examples of Byzantine art.

The gold altarpiece of San Marco, the Pala d'Oro, a portion of which is shown in colour plate 6.8, was commissioned by Doge Ordelafo Falier in 1105.[18] Seen by the congregation from its place in the presbytery of the church, even the casual viewer is impressed with the overall effect of the shining gold altarpiece. From that distance it is impossible to see the true glory of the work, which lays in the amazingly intricate setting of enamels in miniscule cloisonné.

The long history of trade between Venice and the East is reflected in the distinctive architecture of the city. The facades of many of the buildings, with their arched windows and decorative design elements are reminiscent of cities of the East. It has been noted that centres of commerce in Venice like the Rialto market are similar in layout to the city of Aleppo in Syria.[19]

In France too, riches from the East reached the highest echelons of society. King Louis IX built the royal chapel of Sainte-Chapelle to house objects taken from Constantinople: the Crown of Thorns, a portion of the True Cross, and a reliquary of gold made to hold a piece of stone from the Holy Sepulchre.[20] One can view the chapel itself as a life-size reliquary, with its profusion of gold ornament and stained glass windows, reminiscent of church reliquaries in metalwork.

One of the exports of the Crusading world in general was the castle. Castles themselves were not new to Europe. They were built there in the tenth century to protect the lord and his subjects from raids. In northern Europe, they were built mostly of timber and earthwork.[21] But the Crusaders came into contact with the superior Byzantine fortresses built of stone. When it came time to build their own fortifications in the Holy Land, they adopted Byzantine techniques, studied Islamic models, and used their own experience to design and build castles to meet the particular situation they encountered.

In order to build them they had to rely on local builders. These builders replicated what they knew, drawn from the long history of defensive fortifications in the Levant.[22] Innovations to known European models include machicolations and *meurtrières* (arrow slits). Machicolations were parts of the wall surrounding the castle that projected from it and had openings that allowed the defenders to drop missiles on the enemy below.

In Europe, techniques of castle building and siege warfare were brought back by soldiers who had learned them fighting in the Crusades. They were put to use where conflicts involving the control of fortresses was a major factor, as in the war between the Angevin Empire and Capetian France between c. 1180 and c. 1220.[23]

Castles built in the thirteenth century in Europe followed Eastern models by being constructed of stone, and placed on the highest possible location. Round towers often replaced square ones, giving more protection against mining and sapping techniques.[24]

The influence of Islamic and Byzantine art and design continued to be displayed up to and including the Renaissance. While the Renaissance is generally associated with the recovery of Greek and Roman art and literature, the effect of Eastern art dating from the Crusades cannot be denied. Indeed, it was the continuing trade between East and West that has become the subject of much modern scholarship regarding the development of the Renaissance.

As we have already seen, cloth from Islamic lands was valued for both its obvious beauty and superior quality. Its relatively light weight and ease of transport made it a staple of the trade in luxury goods from East to West. In both cultures, displaying and wearing luxury fabrics were a means of communicating one's status and rank.[25] Islamic textiles were used for priestly vestments and church altar cloths. They continued to be a primary object of exchange well after the Crusading period. We see them represented in paintings and sculpture.

When the great sculptor Andrea del Verrocchio cast the bronze statue of David in the fifteenth century, he included what is known as 'pseudo-kufic', 'mock-Arabic', or 'mock-kufic' (pl. 6.9). Artists associated this type of writing with the Holy Land, and thus deemed it appropriate to use in representations of religious figures.[26] As in other works of art we have seen, del Verrocchio appropriated the decorative possibilities of Arabic script to decorate the border of the tunic of the hero.[27] While in this case the writing cannot be deciphered, sometimes the artist was so careful in copying the letters, that it can be translated.

The painting in colour plate 6.10 illustrates the representation of luxurious Islamic cloth in an early Renaissance portrait of the Madonna and Child. In a fascinating combination of Western religiosity and Eastern

6.9 Andrea del Verrocchio, David, *c. 1473-75.*

design elements, the artist combines the Latin inscription *Ave Mater Digna Dei* on the embroidered band of her robe, with pseudo-Arabic on the band of the Christ child's blanket.[28]

Gentile da Fabriano had also seen examples of Islamic brassware. In the Virgin's halo in this picture, he divides the pseudo-Arabic script into sections by inserting rosettes between the script. This exactly follows the pattern on inlaid brass trays and candlesticks imported from Islamic territory (col. pl. 6.11).[29]

Artists incorporate Eastern design elements to give Western works of religious art some of the aura and association with the East. This seems appropriate when one remembers that the place of origin of these biblical religious figures was indeed the East.

The glass portion of the work shown in colour plate 6.12 is a shallow dish which originated in Western Asia, probably Iran, in the ninth or tenth century. The beautiful turquoise coloured bowl is decorated with hares running along its base. The raised images are set off by the gold rim and base, connected by vertical gold straps that frame the lobes containing the hares. The top rim has square panels containing enamel decoration and cabochon set jewels. When works like this came into Europe (or in this case, Constantinople), from the Eastern world, they were often repurposed by adding mountings and jewels. This both preserved and enhanced the luxury status of the item. The enameled plaques in this example date to the tenth or eleventh century and are Byzantine. Alongside the panels with enamels are panels with filigree designs, and these are from Western Europe. It is conjectured that the various elements were put together to

6.13 Le Puy Cathedral (Jane Skelding)

give the object its current form when the bowl came to Venice in the fifteenth century.[30]

The use of such luxury objects in a household was meant to impress guests and augment the status of the owner.

In France, the cathedral in Le Puy-en-Velay (pl. 6.13), owes the striking appearance of its exterior brickwork as much to Spain as to Islamic lands further east. But it shows the willingness of builders to adapt Islamic decoration to enliven the appearance of their ecclesiastical monuments. The alternating bands of dark and white masonry were perhaps copied from the Cordoba Mosque. Here the local black volcanic stone is substituted for the red of Cordoba.[31]

One of the entrance doors to the cathedral was made in about 1150. It shows scenes from the life of Christ, but the scenes are bordered by pseudo-kufic writing which has been translated as 'all power to Allah'. It was only 50 miles from here that Pope Urban II preached the first Crusade in which he characterized the Muslims as

6.15 Le Puy Cathedral, grille

6.14 Dome of the Rock grille, Jerusalem.

an 'infidel race, so justly scorned, which has sunk from the dignity of man and is a vile slave of the devil.'[32] The only explanation for the presence of Arabic writing of 'the infidel' on the doors is the appreciation the artist must have had for the decorative possibilities of the language, coupled with complete ignorance of the meaning of the words.

In yet another example from Le Puy, we can see the similarity of styles in ironwork from both East and West (pls 6.14 and 6.15). One of the works thought to be commissioned by Queen Melisende was the iron grille that surrounded the rock in the Dome of the Rock in Jerusalem. We know that the grille was in place at the Dome of the Rock about 1150.[33] The grille in Le Puy dates from the twelfth century, and is located in the cloister of the cathedral. Besides the similarity of the scrollwork itself, both works have punch marks in the metal. In the case of the grille surrounding the Dome of the

Rock, this would have created a sparkling effect when candles were lit around the enclosure.

The remarkable and beautiful bottle in colour plate 6.16 was made in Syria in the thirteenth century. It illustrates both the proximity of Christian and Islamic communities in the Middle East, and the appreciation for the craftsmanship of Islamic works of art. At first glance, this might appear to be an Islamic enamelled glass vessel. It has the similar shape, decoration, and densely covered surface of other works of glass of the period. But on closer inspection of the scenes, one notices the large cross on top of a building which identifies it as a church. The tall figures on the neck of the vessel have haloes. The figures on the body of the vessel are dressed like monks and deacons. This clearly shows the bottle to be made for a Christian clientele, perhaps a monastery, or an official of the church. The agricultural scenes illustrate the seasons of life and work in a monastery. Only at the bottom of the scenes do we see a border which has typical Islamic decoration of animals in motion along a foliate design.

What the function of this bottle is, and why or for whom it was created remains a mystery. It has been speculated that the vessel was commissioned from an Islamic workshop to mark the appointment of an abbot in a monastery; or perhaps as a gift to a monastery from a Muslim leader. In either case, because of its high cost and exceptional beauty, it would have carried the promise of good will between the two parties.[34]

Objects like this (there are also metalwork examples that were made in Islamic workshops for Christian patrons or export to the West) show the enduring relationship between high quality works produced in Islamic lands and the avid collectors of such works in the West. Neither the religious differences between the two parties, nor the fact of 200 years of fighting between Muslims and Christians seem to have affected the continuity of trade of the two groups with each other.

The Stavelot triptych (col. pl. 6.17) is an excellent illustration of how Western artisans skilfully integrated elements of art from the East into objects of Western veneration. It was assembled to hold pieces of the

True Cross which are housed in the central section. These fragments were probably given to Abbot Wibald (the Abbot of the Benedictine abbey of Stavelot in present-day Belgium) during one of his trips to Constantinople. This reliquary is one of the earliest in the form of a triptych in which the two side panels can be closed over the central panel.[35] Perhaps this form was adopted to echo and reinforce the two triptychs in the centre portion.

The two small triptychs in the central section were made in Byzantium. The background, which is now red velvet, would originally have been gold, studded with jewels.[36] The technique in these small panels is cloisonné: powdered glass is placed into small gold cells, or frames, and then heated to melt the glass. The Byzantines were masters of this technique as can be evidenced by the tiny and intricate depictions of the figures in the panels.

The roundels on the interior of the wings of the triptychs tell two stories. On the left is the story of Constantine's victory over Maxentius in the battle of the Milvian Bridge. Reading from bottom to top: Constantine's dream of the cross; the battle with the soldiers having painted the cross on their shields; his baptism.

On the roundels on the right is the story of Constantine's mother, Helena, and her discovery of the True Cross. From bottom to top: Helena questions the Jews; three crosses are found; the True Cross is identified when it brings a dead man to life.

The roundels telling these stories are made by artists from the region of Mosan, in present-day Belgium. The technique is champlevé enamel, which was the most common method in Europe at the time. With this technique, instead of individual gold cells for the powdered enamel, depressions were gouged out of a metal base and filled with the glass. Before being fired, the ridges thus formed were covered with gold to give the imitative appearance of cloisonné. This technique was less expensive than cloisonné and allowed works to be larger.

The design of the frame itself and the jewels set into the framing elements were done by Mosan craftsmen in the mid-twelfth century. The Byzantine enamels are thought to have been produced around

6.19 Detail, eastern lintel vine scroll from Church of Holy Sepulchre, Jerusalem, 1150 (?). (Collection of the Israel Antiquities Authority)

6.18 Trumeau, Souillac, France.

1100. The act of incorporating the earlier enamels into a later work of art shows the appreciation Western artisans and patrons had for the work of their counterparts in the East. Thus we have an object that combines the expertise of two different traditions to produce a work of unique beauty.

In the *trumeau* of the main entrance to the church in Souillac, France (pl. 6.18), we see what may be described as a three dimensional representation of the inhabited vine scroll, without the unifying presence of the vine. Dated to the twelfth century, this amazing work of art, which was the centre post supporting the tympanum of the church, is a churning, writhing mass of man and animals in the form of a pillar.

6.20 Pisa Baptistry, 1153-1265.

It seems to have some Biblical references, like Abraham sacrificing Isaac, but as a whole, its message is unintelligible, if indeed it does have an overall meaning.[37] When we compare it to the detail of the vine scroll on the lintel of the Church of the Holy Sepulchre (pl. 6.19), we see certain similarities. In both, humans and animals are wrapped together. But when we look again, we are left gaping with the sense of energy and chaos the Souillac sculpture presents. It is as if the Romanesque sculptor used the inhabited vine scroll as a model, then let his imagination run amok.

6.21 Pisa Griffin, Egypt or Spain (?), 11th century.

155

From the eleventh century, Pisa was a sea power with trading interests that extended to the Holy Land. It became wealthy from this trade, and in 1153, started the building of the baptistry as part of the cathedral complex in the city centre (pl. 6.20). It modelled the rotunda of the structure on that of the Church of the Holy Sepulchre in Jerusalem. That structure was itself modelled on the domes of the Byzantine and Islamic worlds. While the baptistry differs from Islamic domes which are usually set on square chambers, by appropriating the design and decoration of its religious monuments, Pisa was celebrating the triumph of Christianity over the infidel. In the eleventh century, Pisa won a naval battle with Islamic forces and brought back a large bronze griffin as part of the booty from that campaign (pl. 6.21). While the griffin was installed on the Pisa cathedral as a sign of their military prowess and dominance,[38] it is somewhat ironic that the griffin is engraved with blessings in Arabic, inadvertently giving an Islamic presence the upper position.

But perhaps this illustrates the symbiotic relationship between the two cultures. Islamic objects are prized for their craftsmanship and beauty while also being booty and as such, considered symbols of Christian and western dominance.

Over time, Western artists studied and copied Islamic artistic techniques and motifs. The city of Venice had a long history of trade and relations with the Islamic east, as we have seen. So it is not surprising to see the influence of Islamic design elements there. The candlestick in plate 6.22 reflects the European adoption of

6.22 Candlestick, Venice, c. 1550, brass and overlaid with silver..

Islamic interlace techniques. It was made in Venice in approximately 1550 of brass and overlaid with silver, in much the same style as the tray in colour plate 6.11. The technique used by the Venetians was called 'damascening', a reference to its Islamic origins and the city of Damascus. The pattern of interlace itself was called 'arabesque', again a tribute to the culture from which it came. We can also see reflected in this piece the Islamic style of overall surface decoration, that *horror vacuii* referred to previously.

The engraved scroll design and interlace pattern are reminiscent of other objects examined in this book. The ivory book covers of the Queen Melisende Psalter contain such designs. And here we can see some of the problems in attributing a design to one culture or another. We find interlace design in the Graeco-Roman tradition. It was adopted and adapted by the Muslims. The nomadic tribes overrunning Europe after the fall of the Roman Empire also brought their tradition of interlace, based on the use of knots to tie their tents and packs. We find examples of interlace in Anglo-Saxon art of the sixth and seventh centuries. Thereafter the development of this artistic motif was most fully realized in the Islamic world. Their knowledge of geometry informed and enhanced the complexity and proportion of the designs. As we have seen in textiles and metalwork, the decorative nature of interlace and calligraphy was highly valued in the west.[39]

Interlace continued to be used with great effect all across Europe for centuries. Just as we see the fluidity with which designs transfer from one medium to another in Queen Melisende's court and all over the East, we see interlace in Europe in fabric (col. pls 6.23 and 6.24), metalwork, illuminated manuscripts, book bindings, and architecture (col. pl. 6.25).

To further examine the transmission of artistic ideas, let us consider the *senmurv*. The *senmurv* is a mythical creature with a dog's head, lion's paws, fish scales, a tail like a peacock, and wings.[40] It comes from the Sasanian tradition where it had three natures that were associated with the three heavens. The lower scales of the fish symbolized the lower heaven; the dog's paws the middle heaven, and

6.26 Brass jug, Iraq or Iran, 9th century. (© The Trustees of the British Museum. All rights reserved)

the bird aspect symbolizing the upper heaven. This creature lived on a tree watered by the seas, which could symbolize the tree of life. It is generally associated with good fortune.[41]

We find images of the *senmurv* on a variety of objects: silks, metalware; and glass. The brass jug in plate 6.26 portrays the *senmurv* in the roundel decorating the body of the jug. This example dates from Iraq or Iran in the ninth century.[42]

Plate 6.27 with the detail of the base shows a variant of the *senmurv* on the base of a bowl made in Iran in the ninth to tenth century. The design has been modified to fit the space available.

In a Byzantine silk from the ninth to tenth century, we find the *senmurv* again, this time modified slightly to have a head that is more lion-like than dog in appearance (col. pl. 6.28). This might allude to the lion-head of the griffin, which was more familiar to the Byzantines.

We find the image again in colour plate 6.29 on a eleventh to twelfth century silk. Because by then, this decorative motif was found over such a large area, encompassing so many cultures, it is difficult to give a definite attribution.[43]

The transmission of the design from one culture to another took place in many ways. Objects with the design were taken as booty from one group conquering another; fantastical creatures like the *senmurv* were popular for decorating a variety of objects; and because originally the design came from the Sasanian royal tradition, it may have been copied to emulate and appropriate the royal connotations.

We can also see the fluidity of the motif from one type of object to another. The size and portability of all the objects shown added to the wide dissemination, not just of this decorative idea, but many others as well.

I use this example to show that design elements are borrowed, used and modified by different cultures. In some cases they lose the original meaning, and a different meaning is attributed to them. In other cases, such as that of the lion and the eagle, the association with royalty and power remains with them. This adds to the interest of the designs, but sometimes makes it difficult to trace the permutations of a specific motif from one culture to another. This is true of design elements flowing from East to West. As the design becomes adopted and modified by a different culture, it becomes part of that culture's decorative milieu, and the origin and meaning it had is lost or changed. Thus the griffin on the top of the Pisa baptistry begins to be thought of as Pisan, not Egyptian or Syrian; the *bacini* that decorate the outside of the cathedral are imitated by Italian potters and lead eventually to the development of what we consider a quintessential Italian tradition of maiolica. Such is the nature of art. Every object has a story. Every story has multiple layers. In uncovering the story is the adventure and the delight.

That the arts of the East had a pervasive and lasting impact on the art of the West is without question. The role of the Crusades in opening the Western mind and markets to the ideas and goods of the East is likewise not in doubt. The role that the court of Queen

6.27 Glass bowl with base medallion of senmurv, Iran, 9-10th century.
(© The al-Sabah Collection, Dar al-Athar al-Islamiyyah, Kuwait)

Melisende played in the dissemination of these ideas and goods is likely to be the subject of necessary research and debate. Given that her power and influence has been ignored, buried, rejected and neglected, any further inquiry will be welcomed.

It is poignant and also instructive that the greatest awareness we have of her is through the art of her time, and especially through the psalter that bears her name. It is perhaps fitting that the psalter itself is such a rich treasure trove of mingling influences and tantalizing connections. It leaves us with unanswered questions about its production and intended recipient. It is a beautiful and somewhat mysterious work that bears long examination and further thought, much like its namesake.

POSTSCRIPT

Having examined the life and times of Queen Melisende, let us return to the ivory covers of the psalter which bears her name. In them, we see the medieval ideals of kingship expressed visually. On the front, scenes from the life of David, serving as a model of princely conduct to every medieval ruler; on the back, the six acts of mercy, delineating the duties of the medieval ruler. The book must have served as a constant reminder to Queen Melisende of what was expected of her. That she was able to reign as a woman in this context of these ideals of kingship tells us much about the kind of person she was.

Her rule and the accomplishments we have noted in the previous chapters are even more remarkable when we consider the remarks of Bernard of Clairvaux quoted previously in Chapter 1.

Bernard sets out the impossible: do great things; act as a man and king though you are a woman and a queen; be strong though you are weak; acknowledge you are powerless, changeable, and incapable in matters of diplomacy and business, yet make people believe you are so skilled at these that they will think you a king rather than a queen.

Such ridiculous and contradictory requirements are not unfamiliar to women today. Powerful women manoeuvring in the treacherous waters of gender identity in the twelfth century or the twenty-first century have faced a daunting task.

As the quote from Bernard of Clairvaux points out, women in the twelfth century were perceived as, and expected to play the role of the weak vessel. Yet Melisende, chosen by fate or divine providence (as she must have felt) to fulfil a higher calling, could not be constantly calling attention to her weakness as a woman, but would have to, as

Bernard pointed out, 'act like a man'. But only within the proscribed limitations: she must not 'be' like a man. She must remember her place and use her feminine nature to convince and cajole others to her aims, but not to the extent she is seen as a sex object, or even using her sex, as that would have been outside the acceptable moral boundaries of her time, rank, and station.

Indeed, parallels with the dilemmas facing Queen Melisende and those facing women of rank and power in our own time can easily be made. In a twelfth-century way, she dealt with the same issues: How do you show yourself strong enough to be a leader, yet maintain society's expectations of female behaviour? If you cry, you are assailed by both ends of the political spectrum—both criticized for being weak and hailed for showing your 'feminine side', your vulnerability. If you stubbornly hold to a course of action, or criticize an opponent, you are unfeminine, or worse. You are judged not only by your beliefs, but by what you are wearing and your smile. Of course we do not expect our male rulers to cry and they are not called upon to prove their vulnerability, nor do we subject them to analysis of their sartorial choices, or facial expressions. So this double standard traps women and keeps them walking the tightrope between public expectations and effective public service, and determines how they are treated, not only in their own time, but by history as well.

Queen Melisende was caught in a similar bind. With the scarcity of information about her person and her rule, it is both tempting and dangerous to project the current dilemmas of women in power onto her. And yet, from current experience, we can also appreciate the delicate position she was in and admire her for navigating her course in power so skilfully.

According to evidence of her behaviour (towards Fulk after her father died, and her treatment of her son) she seems to have been a strong-willed woman, to say the least. That must have made it even harder for her to tolerate the limitations placed on her by her sex. Did she take her cues from the battle between the vices and virtues on the front cover of her psalter, where fortitude triumphs over avarice and sobriety over luxury? If we interpret sobriety as acceptance and luxury as self-pity, then it may be so. She certainly had fortitude and perseverance. Using these inner strengths she proved to be an effective and successful ruler. She also knew how to use her relationships with the other nobles and the clergy to establish a power base. It is clear she was politically shrewd and talented administratively. She made the most of the obligations and opportunities presented to her.

What if Queen Melisende had acquiesced in all matters to the male power figures in her life: her husband after her marriage; the men vying for power after her husband's death; her son on his fifteenth birthday? Would Fulk and his followers have been able to unite the kingdom and rule effectively, or would there have been civil war between the Anjou contingent and the descendents of the first crusaders, further weakening the kingdom and allowing the Muslims an early and complete victory? The danger lurked again after Fulk's death. Without the strength of her character and the establishment of her power, the kingdom once again might have plunged into disastrous civil war. And was her son really ready to rule a kingdom at the young age of fifteen? Did not his mother's experience in administration allow him to mature and develop as a man before taking over the kingdom? Was not the accepted authority of Queen Melisende the one thing that allowed continuity as these events transpired in the young and delicate Crusader kingdom? Of course we cannot know the answers to these questions, but the questions themselves help us appreciate the position of Queen Melisende and the decisions that she made.

As we come full circle then, back to the psalter that bears her name, we can see more clearly the parallels between that book's ivory covers and the life of Melisende. Just as the psalter reflects the blending of artistic styles of three cultures, so Melisende herself is a blending of cultures. As the psalter reflects how rulers were expected to behave, so Queen Melisende sought to embody the virtues illustrated there. As the images are intertwined and interrelated, so Queen Melisende's life is intertwined and related with that of the crusader states. And finally, both queen and psalter leave us with more questions than answers.

That such a fascinating and powerful woman can be so effectively buried and forgotten is deeply troubling. I suggest to the reader that there are many other such powerful women in history who have likewise been hidden. It is my hope that this will be but one of the books dealing with Queen Melisende's life, and that other women unknown to us from history will be brought out of the shadows by future writers.

GLOSSARY

Anastasis   (Gr., 'resurrection'): representation of Christ bursting the gates of hell and releasing Old Testament figures said to have believed in him before the Incarnation; the Easter image of the Orthodox Church.

caliph   (Arabic *khalifa*): 'deputy'/'successor', commander of the Islamic community (theoretically) combining both religious and political functions.

Deesis   (Gr., 'entreaty'): work used in medieval Byzantium for a representation of Christ flanked by the intercessory figures of the Virgin and Saint John the Baptist; since the nineteenth century, the conventional designation of this image.

hyperpyron   (Gr. 'super-refined'): the name given to the coin in use in the latter Middle Ages, replacing the *solidus* as the empire's gold coinage. Emperor Alexius I Comnenus overhauled the Byzantine coinage system and introduced this new gold coin.

incipit   (Lat., 'here begins'): formula that introduces a scriptural text; the page on which it appears is often given special decoration.

icon   (Gr., 'image'): any image of a sacred personage; the term is used most often to indicate a representation on a portable panel.

interstices   the area between shapes.

kufic   a form of Arabic script.

mihrab   a recess or niche on the *qibla* wall.

minaret   (Anglicisation of the Arabic *manara*): in theory a tower from which the call to prayer was given. In practice, minarets were used for a variety of purposes and, in particular, the multiple minarets of large mosques often have a purely decorative function.

niello   a black metallic substance, consisting of silver, copper, lead, and sulphur, with which an incised design or ground is filled to produce an ornamental effect on metal.

panegyris   (Gr., 'festival'): periodic local or international religious and commercial fair.

Pantocrator   (Gr., 'all-holy'): epithet of God as well as of the individual persons of the Trinity; designates the best-known type of image of Christ, bearded and represented frontally, blessing with his right hand while he holds the Gospel book in his left; a bust of Christ Pantokrator often formed the centre of Byzantine dome decoration.

qibla   the direction of prayer, towards Mecca.

Shi'a   the religious party who support the claim of Ali (cousin of the Prophet Muhammad) and his descendants to leadership of the Islamic community. There are several branches of the Shi'a faith, which differ from one another in supporting different chains of succession.

Sunni   the adjective applied to the broad body of 'orthodox' Muslims who hold that succession to leadership of the Islamic community after the death of the Prophet was elective rather than hereditary (thus distinguishing them from Shi'a Muslims).

staurotheke   (Gr. 'cross chest'): reliquary made to contain a fragment of the True Cross.

NOTES TO THE TEXT

INTRODUCTION

1   A psalter is a book based around the Psalms of King David from the Old Testament. Many, like the Queen Melisende Psalter, also contained parts of the New Testament, a calendar, and prayers.

1
FORGOTTEN QUEEN

1   H E Mayer, 'Studies in the History of Queen Melisende of Jerusalem', *Dumbarton Oaks Papers*, 26 (1972), Washington, p. 99.
2   B Hamilton, 'Women in the Crusader States: the queens of Jerusalem (1100-1190), *Medieval Women*, ed. D Baker, Oxford, 1978, p. 147.
3   M Baldwin, ed., *A History of the Crusades*, Vol. 1, University of Pennsylvania, 1958, p. 302.
4   C Tyerman, *God's War*, Harvard University Press, 2006, p. 186.
5   *Ibid.*, p. 186.
6   J La Monte, *Feudal monarchy in the Latin Kingdom of Jerusalem, 1100 to 1291*, Cambridge, Mass., 1932, p. 8.
7   S Schein, 'Women in the Crusader Period', *Knights of the Holy Land*, ed. S Rozenberg, Israel, 1999, pp. 61-7. esp. p. 63.
8   S Runciman, *History of the Crusades*, vol. II, Cambridge, 1952, pp. 177-8.
9   William of Tyre, *A History*, II, book 14, ch. 1.
10 C Tyerman, *God's War*, p. 207.
11 H E Mayer, *The Crusades*, 1972, p. 80.
12 B Kühnel, *Crusader Art of the Twelfth Century*, Berlin, 1994, p. 80.
13 F Gabrieli, *Arab Historians of the Crusades*, Los Angeles, 1969, p. 40.
14 J Folda, *The Art of the Crusades in the Holy Land, 1098-1187*, Cambridge, 1995, p. 114.
15 For a full discussion of the history and circumstances, see H Mayer, 'The Succession to Baldwin II of Jerusalem: English Impact on the East', *Dumbarton Oaks Papers*, 39, (1985), Washington, pp. 139-47.

16 Orderic Vitalis, *Ecclesiastical History*, 6.390-93.

17 William of Tyre, Book 2, p. 72.

18 J Phillips, *Holy Warriors*, pp. 62-67.

19 Mayer, 'Queen Melisende', p. 110.

20 William of Tyre, p. 710.

21 N Hodgson, Women, Crusading and the Holy Land in Historical Narrative, Suffolk, 2007, p. 135.

22 B Kühnel, *Crusader Art of the Twelfth Century*, p. 81.

23 H E Mayer,' Studies in the History of Queen Melisende of Jerusalem', p. 110.

24 B Kühnel, p. 85.

25 This discussion is based on observations by the author and selective use of Bianca Kühnel's extensive and in-depth analysis of the Queen Melisende Psalter covers in *Crusader Art of the Twelfth Century; A Geographical, an Historical, or an Art Historical Notion?*, Berlin 1994.

26 B Kühnel, pp. 69, 73, 91, 82.

27 *Ibid.*, p. 82.

28 William of Tyre, Book 15, ch. 27.

29 J Folda, *The Art of the Crusaders in the Holy Land, 1098-1187*, p. 174.

30 William of Tyre, II, Book 16, ch. 3.

31 *The Letters of St Bernard of Clairvaux*, trans. B S James, London, 1953, pp. 345-8.

32 William of Tyre, II, Book 16, ch.3, pp. 139-40.

33 H E Mayer, "Studies in the History of Queen Melisende of Jerusalem", p. 166.

34 *Ibid.*, p. 169.

35 William of Tyre, Book 16, ch. 3.

36 *Ibid.*, Book 18, ch. 27.

37 *Ibid.*, Book 18, ch. 32, p. 850.

38 J Folda, p. 324.

2

The Crusades

1 J Singman, *Daily Life in Medieval Europe*, Connecticut, 1999, pp. 11-12.

2 J Phillips, *Holy Warriors*, London, 2009, p. 4.

3 M Adamson, *Food in Medieval Times,* Connecticut, 2004, p. 30.

4 D Whitton, 'The Society of Northern Europe in the High Middle Ages' in *The Oxford Illustrated History of Medieval Europe,* G Holmes, ed., Oxford 1988, p. 128.

5 J Singman, *Daily Life in Medieval Europe*, p. 100.

6 *Ibid.*, pp. 30-4.

7 *Ibid.*, pp. 50-51.

8 M Adamson, *Food in Medieval Times,* p. 2-3.

9 This information and the following discussion comes from Melitta Weiss Adamson, *Food in Medieval Times*, *op. cit.*, chapter 4; and Joseph and Frances Gies, *Life in a Medieval Castle*, New York, 1974, ch. 6.

10 J Singman, *Daily Life in Medieval Europe*, p. 85.

11 M Adamson, *Food in Medieval Times*, p. 160.

12 R Stalley, *Early Medieval Architecture*, Oxford, 1999, pp. 130-2.

13 H Janson, *History of Art*, New York, 1962, p. 209.

14 U Geese, 'Romanesque sculpture', in *Romanesque*, R Toman, ed., Cologne, 2004, p. 328.

15 T Asbridge, *The First Crusade, A New History*, Oxford, 2004, p. 6.

16 J Phillips, *Holy Warriors*, pp. 12-13. Also Gies, Marriage and Family in the Middle Ages, 1987, p. 135.

17 J Prawer, *The World of the Crusaders*, New York, 1972, p. 14.

18 J Herrin, *Byzantium*, p. 220-1.

19 Robert the Monk's account, in D Munro, 'Urban and the Crusaders', *Translations and Reprints from the Original Sources of European History,* Vol.1: 2, Philadelphia 1895, pp. 5-8.

20 J Riley-Smith, *The Atlas of the Crusades*, New York, 1991, p. 44.

21 Fulcher of Chartres, *A History of the Expedition to Jerusalem, 1095-1127*, trans. Frances Rila Ryan, ed. H Fink, University of Tennessee, 1969, p. 67.

22 J Prawer, *The World of the Crusaders*, p. 17.

23 Fulcher of Chartres, *A History of the Expedition to Jerusalem, 1095-1127*, trans. Frances Rila Ryan, ed. H. Fink, University of Tennessee, 1969, pp. 66-7; O Thatcher, E H McNeal, eds., *A Source Book for Medieval History*, pp. 514-15.

24 *Ibid.*, pp. 66-7.

25 T Asbridge, *The First Crusade*, p. 86.

26 J Prawer, *World of the Crusaders*, pp. 21-22.

27 J Riley-Smith, *The First Crusaders*, p. 170.

28 T Asbridge, *The First Crusade*, p. 53.

29 *Ibid.*, p. 65.

30 *Ibid.*, p. 79.

31 J Singman, *Daily Life in Medieval Europe*, p. 174.

32 J Herrin, Byzantium, p. 18.

33 *Gesta Francorum*, Albert of Aix, II, 28, pp. 320-1.

34 S Runciman, *History of the Crusades*, vol. I, Cambridge, 1951, pp. 180-1.

35 *Ibid.*, p. 208.

36 *Ibid.*, p. 276.

37 *Gesta Francorum*, X, 38, Raymond of Aguilers, XX, 300; pp. 204-6.

38 A Maalouf, *The Crusades Through Arab Eyes*, p. 265.

39 S Runciman, *History of the Crusades*, vol. I, p. 287.

40 N Kedar, 'The Figurative Western Lintel of the Church of the Holy Sepulchre in Jerusalem', The *Meeting of Two Worlds: Cultural Exchange between East and West during the Period of the Crusades,* Kalamazoo, 1986, pp. 123-31.

41 D Munro, 'Urban and the Crusaders', *Translations and Reprints from the Original Sources of European History,* Vol.1:2, Philadelphia 1895, pp. 5-8.

42 A Maalouf, *The Crusades Through Arab Eyes*, London, 1983, p. 39.

43 *Ibid.*, p. 51.

44 Raymond of Aguilers, p. 150.

45 A Maalouf, *The Crusades Through Arab Eyes*, prologue, ii.

46 A Bridge, *The Crusades*, New York, 1982, p. 115.

47 S Runciman, *History of the Crusades*, vol. I, p. 293.
48 J Riley-Smith, *The Atlas of the Crusaders*, p. 36.
49 S Runciman, *History of the Crusades*, vol. II, p. 316.

3

RICHES AND RITUAL:
THE BYZANTINE EMPIRE

1 J Norwich, *A Short History of Byzantium*, New York, 1997, pp. 6-7.
2 *Ibid.*, p. 7.
3 *Ibid.*, pp. 11-14.
4 J Herrin, *Byzantium*, London, 2007, p. 25.
5 W Durant, *The Story of Civilization; The Age of Faith*, New York, 1950, p. 5.
6 B Rosenwein, *A Short History of the Middle Ages*, Toronto, 2004, pp. 50-51 and 56.
7 R Irwin, *Islamic Art in Context*, New York, 1997, pp. 20-25.
8 S Vryonis, 'Byzantine Society and Civilization' in *The Glory of Byzantium,* ed. H Evans and W Wixom, New York, 1997, p. 5.
9 J Herrin, *Byzantium*, p. 18.
10 P Magdalino, 'The Medieval Empire (780-1204)', *The Oxford History of Byzantium*, C Mango, ed., Oxford, 2002, p. 179.
11 J Herrin, *Byzantium*, p. 19.
12 R Ousterhout, 'Secular Architecture', in *The Glory of Byzantium*, p. 196.
13 A Comnena, *The Alexiad*, trans. by E Sewter, London, 1969, p. 328.
14 J Prawer, *The World of the Crusaders*, New York, 1972, p. 22.
15 J Herrin, *Byzantium*, p. 45.
16 A Comnena, *The Alexiad*, p. 111.
17 W Metcalf, in *The Glory of Byzantium*, p. 216.
18 H Maguire, 'Images of the Court', in *The Glory of Byzantium*, p. 183.
19 S Vryonis, 'Byzantine Society and Civilization', p. 6.
20 T Mathews, 'Religious Organization and Church Architecture, in *The Glory of Byzantium*, p. 21.
21 T Mathews, 'Religious Organization and Church Architecture', p. 21.
22 In this picture, Hagia Sophia is shown in its present day form. The tall towers, minarets, were added by the Muslims after the fall of Constantinople to those forces in 1453.
23 M Stokstad, *Medieval Art*, Boulder, Colorado, 2004, p. 52.
24 *Ibid.*, p. 52.
25 R Cormack, *Byzantine Art*, Oxford, 2000, p. 22.
26 M Stokstad, *Medieval Art*, p. 54.
27 http://www.focusmm.com/civilization/hagia/history.htm, 2/18/11.
28 M Stokstad, *Medieval Art*, p. 54.
29 T Mathews, 'Religious Organization and Church Architecture', p. 25.
30 *Idem.*
31 www.traditionaliconogaphy.com/theology.asp.

32 R Nelson, 'Where God Walked and Monks Pray', *Icons from Sinai*, R Nelson and K Collins, eds., Los Angeles, 2006, p. 27.

33 T Mathews, 'Early Icons of the Holy Monastery of Saint Catherine at Sinai', *Icons from Sinai*, p. 54.

34 S Boyd, in *Glory of Byzantium*, pp. 178-9.

35 S Vryonis, 'Byzantine Society and Civilization', p. 10.

36 D Walker, in *Glory of Byzantium*, pp. 415-6.

37 P Soucek, 'Byzantium and the Islamic East', *Glory of Byzantium*, 1997, p. 403.

38 *Ibid*. p. 404

39 I Kalavrezou, in *Glory of Byzantium*, p. 251.

40 W Wixom, in *Glory of Byzantium*, pp. 246-7.

41 E Maguire, 'Ceramic Arts of Everyday Life', in *Glory of Byzantium*, p. 255.

42 E Maguire, in *Glory of Byzantium*, p. 263.

43 J Herrin, *Byzantium*, p. 261.

44 J Phillips, *Holy Warriors*, p. 16.

45 *Ibid.*, p. 258.

46 R Cormack, *Byzantine Art*, p. 180.

4

ENCOUNTERING THE ISLAMIC WORLD

1 A Maalouf, *The Crusades Through Arab Eyes*, London, 1983, pp. 1-56.

2 A Hourani, *A History of the Arab Peoples*, Cambridge, 1991, pp. 14-5.

3 *Ibid.*, p. 20.

4 *Ibid.*, pp. 147-9.

5 W Ball, *Syria*, London, 2006, p. 37.

6 A Hourani, *A History of the Arab Peoples*, p. 22.

7 *Ibid.*, p. 23.

8 W Ball, *Syria*, p. 35.

9 *Ibid.*, pp. 37-39.

10 T Asbridge, *The Crusades*, New York, 2010, pp. 21-22.

11 *Ibid.*, p. 21-22.

12 C Hillenbrand, *The Crusades: Islamic Perspectives*, Edinburgh, 1999, p. 44.

13 *Ibid.*, p. 303.

14 *Ibid.*, p. 267.

15 B Rosenwein, *A Short History of the Middle Ages*, p. 151.

16 W Ball, *Syria*, p. 33.

17 S Vryonis, 'Byzantine Society and Civilization', *The Glory of Byzantium*, eds. H Evans, W Wixom, New York, 1997, p. 17.

18 R Irwin, *Islamic Art in Context*, New York, 1997, pp. 24-27.

19 C Hillenbrand, *The Crusades: Islamic Perspectives*, Edinburgh, 1999, p. 270.

20 *Ibid.*, p. 274.

21 A Maalouf, *The Crusades Through Arab Eyes*, pp. 37-40.

22 *Ibid.*, pp. 284-5.

23 J Prawer, *The World of the Crusaders*, p. 26.
24 Not to be confused with the Abbey of the Dormition on Mt Zion, built much later.
25 B O'Kane, *Treasures of Islam*, London, 2007, p. 34.
26 C Hillenbrand, *The Crusades: Islamic Perspectives*, p. 286.
27 R Hillenbrand, *Islamic Art and Architecture,* Edinburgh, 1999, p. 25.
28 R Hillenbrand, *Islamic Art and Architecture*, p. 25.
29 B O'Kane, *Treasures of Islam*, p. 37.
30 *Ibid.*, pp. 27-8.
31 *Ibid.*, p. 29
32 R Ettinghausen and O Grabar, *The Art and Architecture of Islam, 650-1250*, New Haven and London, 1987, p. 44.
33 *Ibid.*, p. 40.
34 J Allan, *Islamic Ceramics*, Oxford, 1991, p. 4.
35 R Irwin, *Islamic Art in Context*, p. 208-9.
36 R Hillenbrand, *Islamic Art and Architecture*, p. 55.
37 R Ettinghausen and O Grabar, *The Art and Architecture of Islam*, p. 230.
38 Allan, *Islamic Ceramics*, p. 18.
39 S Carboni and D Whitehouse, *Glass of the Sultans*, New Haven and London, 2001, p. 93.
40 *Ibid.*, p. 73.
41 R Hillenbrand*, Islamic Art and Architecture*, p. 96.
42 R Ettinghausen and O Grabar, *The Art and Architecture of Islam,* p. 334.
43 B O'Kane, *Treasures of Islam*, pp. 108-10.
44 R Hillenbrand, *Islamic Art and Architecture*, p. 48.
45 R Irwin, *Islamic Art in Context*, p. 157.
46 R Ward, *Islamic Metalwork*, British Museum Press, 1993, p. 9.
47 J Allan, *Islamic Ceramics*, p. 4.
48 R Irwin, *Islamic Art in Context*, p. 180.
49 R Hillenbrand, *Islamic Art and Architecture*, p. 66.
50 R Irwin, *Islamic Art in Context*, p. 181.
51 B O'Kane, *Treasures of Islam*, p. 53.
52 R Ettinghausen and O Grabar, *The Art and Architecture of Islam,* p. 337.
53 *Ibid.*, p. 337.
54 R Ward, *Islamic Metalwork*, p. 74.
55 R Hillenbrand, *Islamic Art and Architecture*, p. 66.
56 E Atil, ed., *Islamic Art and Patronage: Treasures from Kuwait*, the Al Sabah Collection, New York, 1990.
57 C Perry, Foreword in L Zaouali, *Medieval Cuisine of the Islamic World*, Berkeley, 2007, p. ix.
58 L Zaouali, *Medieval Cuisine of the Islamic World*, p. 6.
59 *Ibid.*, p. 12.
60 *Ibid.*, p. 52.

5
Power and Patronage

1 J Singman, *Daily Life in Medieval Europe*, p. 14.
2 A Maalouf, *On Identity*, London, 2000, p. 3.
3 See H E Mayer, 'Studies in the History of Queen Melisende of Jerusalem', p. 99.
4 In this I am sincerely indebted to the work of Jaroslav Folda, whose book, *The Art of the Crusaders in the Holy Land, 1098-1187*, has been an invaluable resource. This volume remains unsurpassed in its detailed and comprehensive treatment of the time and place under consideration.
5 Mayer, 'Studies', p. 98.
6 Folda, *The Art of the Crusaders*, p. 247.
7 B Kühnel, *Crusader Art of the Twelfth Century*, p. 24.
8 *Ibid.*, p. 20.
9 *Ibid.*, p. 20.
10 Folda, *The Art of the Crusaders*, p. 203.
11 *Ibid.*, p. 136.
12 *Ibid.*, p. 204.
13 *Ibid.*, p. 225.
14 M Lindner, 'Topography and Iconography in 12th-century Jerusalem', *The Horns of Hattin*, ed. B Z Kedar, Jerusalem, 1992, pp. 81-98.
15 N Kedar, 'The Figurative Western Lintel of the Church of the Holy Sepulcher in Jerusalem', *The Meeting of Two Worlds: Cultural Exchange between East and West during the Period of the Crusades,* Kalamazoo, 1986, pp. 123-31.
16 It must be said that Folda, in *The Art of the Crusades in the Holy Land, 1098-1187*, does not agree with this reading of the lintel, and prefers Lindner's interpretation. See footnote 82, p. 540, and pp. 226-7.
17 B Kühnel, *Crusader Art of the Twelfth Century*, p. 43.
18 *Ibid.*, p. 43
19 Folda, *The Art of the Crusades,* p. 227.
20 Even though altered by fire, earthquake and subsequent renovations, the basic form of the church today is the same as in the 12th century.
21 B Kühnel, *Crusader Art of the Twelfth Century,* p. 23.
22 *Ibid.*, p. 22.
23 Folda, *The Art of the Crusades*, p. 228.
24 Folda, *The Art of the Crusades*, p. 137
25 H Buchtal, *Miniature Painting in the Latin Kingdom of Jerusalem*, Oxford, 1957, p. 2.
26 Folda, *The Art of the Crusades*, p. 155.
27 H Buchtal, *Miniature Painting in the Latin Kingdom of Jerusalem*, p. 12.
28 http://www.newadvent.org/cathen/04517a.htm, 4/2/11.
29 Folda, *Art of the Crusaders*, p. 167.
30 *Ibid.*, p. 100.
31 *Ibid.*, pp. 99-100.
32 *Ibid.*, pp. 97-8.
33 C Hillenbrand, *Islamic Perspectives*, p. 389.

34 J Prawer, *The World of the Crusaders*, p. 145.
35 S Runciman, *A History of the Crusades*, vol. II, p. 318.
36 *Ibid.*, p. 318.
37 J Prawer, *The World of the Crusaders,* p. 84.
38 *Ibid.*, p. 88.
39 *The Holy Land*, p. 22.
40 J Prawer, *The World of the Crusaders*, p. 85.
41 S Runciman, *A History of the Crusades*, vol. II, p. 316.
42 C Hillenbrand, *Islamic Perspectives*, p. 388.
43 *Islamic Art and Patronage, Treasures from Kuwait*, 1990.
44 R Ward, *Islamic Metalwork*, p. 54.
45 S Carboni and D Whitehouse, *Glass of the Sultans*, p. 220.
46 *Ibid.*, p. 124.
47 R Ettinghausen and O Grabar, *The Art and Architecture of Islam,* p. 191.
48 R Hillenbrand, *Islamic Art and Architecture*, p. 84.
49 S Carboni and D Whitehouse, *Glass of the Sultans,* p. 139.
50 J Prawer, *World of the Crusaders*, p. 87.
51 S Runciman, *A History of the Crusades*, vol. II, p. 317.
52 A Gonosova, in *Glory of Byzantium*, p. 226.

6

BEYOND THE COURT OF
QUEEN MELISENDE

1 J Prawer, *The World of the Crusaders*, pp. 38-50.
2 J Folda, *The Art of the Crusaders*, p. 480.
3 J Prawer, *The World of the Crusaders*, p. 140.
4 *Ibid.*, p. 141.
5 *Ibid.*, p. 143.
6 *Ibid.*, p. 144.
7 R Ettinghausen and O Grabar, *The Art and Architecture of Islam*, p. 362.
8 H Evans and W Wixom, eds., *The Glory of Byzantium*, p. 226.
9 C Bornstein, 'The Latin West and the Courtly Arts of Byzantium and Islam', in *The Meeting of Two Worlds: the Crusades and the Mediterranean Context*, C Olds, ed., University of Michigan, 1981, p. 18.
10 H A Klein, ed., *Sacred Gifts and Worldly Treasures*, Cleveland, 2007, p. 147.
11 R Mack, *Bazaar to Piazza*, Berkeley, 2002, p. 3.
12 *Ibid.*, p. 96.
13 J Allan, *Islamic Ceramics*, Oxford, 1991, p. 12.
14 P Soucek, 'Artistic Exchange in the Mediterranean Context', in *The Meeting of Two Worlds*, Kalamazoo, 1981, pp. 15-6.
15 J Herrin, *Byzantium*, p. 262.
16 *Ibid.*, p. 264.

17 R. Cormack, *Byzantine Art.*, Oxford, 2000, p. 187.

18 J Herrin, *Byzantium*, p. 205.

19 J Brotton, *The Renaissance Bazaar*, Oxford, 2002, p. 40.

20 R Cormack, *Byzantium*, p. 187.

21 J and F Gies, *Life in a Medieval Castle*, New York, 1974, p. 31.

22 W Ball, *Syria*, London, 2006, p. 64.

23 H Kennedy, *Crusader Castles*, Cambridge, 1994, p. 186.

24 J and F Gies, *Life in a Medieval Castle*, New York, 1974, pp. 27-8.

25 R Mack, *Bazaar to Piazza*, p. 27.

26 *Ibid.*, p. 52.

27 R Irwin, *Islamic Art*, p. 228.

28 R Mack, *Bazaar to Piazza*, p. 62.

29 *Ibid.*, p. 65.

30 S Carboni and D Whitehouse, *Glass of the Sultans*, p. 188.

31 R Stalley, *Early Medieval Architecture*, p. 188.

32 A Petzold, *Romanesque Art*, New York, 1995, p. 146.

33 J Folda, *The Art of the Crusades* pp. 136-7.

34 Carboni and Whitehouse, *Glass of the Sultans*, pp. 242-45.

35 A Petzold, *Romanesque Art*, p. 63.

36 H Evans and W Wixom, eds., *The Glory of Byzantium*, p. 462.

37 A Petzold, *Romanesque Art*, p. 164.

38 *Ibid.*, p. 146.

39 A Gruber, 'Interlace', in *The Renaissance and Mannerism in Europe*, ed. by A Gruber, Paris, 1993 pp. 24-5.

40 *Glory*, p. 224.

41 B O'Kane, *Iconography of Islamic Art*, p. 119.

42 R Ward, *Islamic Metalwork*, p. 38.

43 *Glory*, p. 416.

BIBLIOGRAPHY

Albert of Aix. *Gesta Francorum*, II, 28.

Allan, J. 'The Influence of the Metalwork of the Arab Mediterranean on that of Medieval Europe', *The Arab Influence in Medieval Europe*, ed. D Agius, R Hitchcock, Reading, 1994, pp. 44-62.

Allan, J. *Islamic Ceramics*, Oxford, 1991.

Armstrong, K. *Muhammad*, London, 2006.

Asbridge, T. *The First Crusade, A New History*, Oxford, 2004.

Atil, E., ed. *Islamic Art and Patronage: Treasures from Kuwait*, the Al Sabah Collection, New York, 1990.

Atroshenko, V I, Collins, J. *The Origins of the Romanesque: Near Eastern Influences on European Art 4th-12th Centuries*, London, 1985.

Bagrow, L. *History of Cartography*, London, 1964.

Bahat, D. *Illustrated Atlas of Jerusalem*, New York, 1989.

Baldwin, M. ed. *A History of the Crusades*, Vol. 1, Univ. of Pennsylvania, 1958.

Ball, W. *Syria*, London, 2006.

Bernard of Clairvaux. *The Letters of St. Bernard of Clairvaux*, trans. B S James, London, 1953.

Biddle, M. *The Tomb of Christ*, Gloucestershire, 1999.

Bitel, L M. *Women in Early Medieval Europe, 400-1100*, Cambridge, 2002.

Bornstein, C. 'The Latin West and the Courtly Arts of Byzantium and Islam', in *The Meeting of Two Worlds: the Crusades and the Mediterranean Context*, C. Olds, ed., Univ. of Michigan, 1981.

Bridge, Antony. *The Crusades*, UK, 1980.

Brotton, J. *The Renaissance Bazaar*, Oxford, 2002.

Buchtal, H. *Miniature Painting in the Latin Kingdom of Jerusalem*, Oxford, 1957.

Carboni, S, and Whitehouse, D. *Glass of the Sultans*, New Haven and London, 2001.

Carboni, S. *Glass from Islamic Lands*, New York, 2001.

Charanis, P. *Armenians in the Byzantine Empire*, Lisboa, 1963.

Comnena, Anna. *The Alexiad*, trans. by E Sewter, London, 1969.

Cormack, R. *Byzantine Art*, Oxford, 2000.

Daneshvari, Abbas. 'Cup, Branch, Bird and Fish: An iconographical Study of the Figure Holding a Cup and Branch Flanked by a Bird and a Fish', in *The Iconography of Islamic Art*, ed. B O'Kane, Edinburgh, 2005.

Durant, Will. *The Story of Civilization; The Age of Faith*, New York, 1950.

Ettinghausen, R, and Grabar, O. *The Art and Architecture of Islam, 650-1250*, New Haven and London, 1987.

Evans, H. 'The Armenians', in *The Glory of Byzantium*, ed. H Evans and W Wixom, New York, 1997.

Folda, J. 'Images of Queen Melisende in Manuscripts of William of Tyre's History of Outremer: 1250-1300', *Gesta*, Vol. XXXII/2, New York, 1993, pp. 97-112.

Folda, J. 'Reflections on Art in Crusader Jerusalem about the time of the Second Crusade: c. 1140-c. 1150', in *The Second Crusade and the Cistercians*, ed. M Gervers, New York, 1992, pp.171-182.

Folda, J. *The Art of the Crusades in the Holy Land, 1098-1187*, Cambridge, 1995.

Fulcher of Chartres. *A History of the Expedition to Jerusalem, 1095-1127*, trans. by Frances Rila Ryan, ed. by H Fink, University of Tennessee, 1969.

Gabrieli, F. *Arab Historians of the Crusades*, Los Angeles, 1969.

Geese, U. 'Romanesque sculpture', in *Romanesque*, R Toman, ed., Cologne, 2004.

Gies, J, and F. *Life in a Medieval Castle*, New York, 1974.

Gies, Joseph and Frances. *Marriage and Family in the Middle Ages*, New York, 1987.

Gonosova, A. Contributor to the catalog, *Glory of Byzantium*, ed. H Evans and W Wixom, New York 1997.

Grabar, O. 'Patterns and Ways of Cultural Exchange', in *The Meeting of Two Worlds: Cultural Exchange Between East and West during the Period of the Crusades*, ed. V P Goss, Kalamazoo, 1986.

Gruber, A. 'Interlace', in *The Renaissance and Mannerism in Europe*, ed. by A Gruber, Paris, 1993.

Hamilton, B. 'Women in the Crusader States: the Queens of Jerusalem (1100–1190)', Medieval *Women*, ed. D Baker, Oxford, 1978.

Herrin, Judith. *Byzantium*, London, 2007.

Hillenbrand, C. *The Crusades: Islamic Perspectives*, Edinburgh, 1999.

Hillenbrand, R. *Islamic Art and Architecture*, London, 1999.

Hodgson, N. *Women, Crusading and the Holy Land in Historical Narrative*, UK, 2007.

Honeycutt, L. 'Female Succession and the Language of Power in the Writings of Twelfth-Century Churchmen', *Medieval Queenship*, ed. J C Parsons, New York, 1993.

Hourani, A. *A History of the Arab Peoples*, Cambridge, 1991.

Irwin, R. *Islamic Art in Context*, New York, 1997.

Janson, H. *History of Art*, New York, 1962.

Jones, Terry. *Medieval Lives*, London, 2004.

Kalavrezou, I. 'Luxury Objects', in *Glory of Byzantium,* ed. H Evans and W Wixom, New York, 1997.

Kedar, N. 'The Figurative Western Lintel of the Church of the Holy Sepulchre in Jerusalem', The *Meeting of Two Worlds: Cultural Exchange between East and West during the Period of the Crusades, ed. V.P. Goss,* Kalamazoo, 1986, pp. 123-131.

Kennedy, H. *Crusader Castles*, Cambridge, 1994.

Klein, H A, ed. *Sacred Gifts and Worldly Treasures*, Cleveland, 2007.

Kuhnel, B. *Crusader Art of the Twelfth Century*, Berlin, 1994.

La Monte, J. *Feudal monarchy in the Latin Kingdom of Jerusalem, 1100 to 1291*, Cambridge, Mass., 1932.

Lambert, S. 'Queen or Consort: Rulership and Politics in the Latin Eat, 1118-1228', in *Queens and Queenship in Medieval Europe*, ed. A Duggan, London, 1995.

Lasko, P. *Ars Sacra 800–1200*, London, 1972.

Lindner, M. 'Topography and Iconography in 12th-century Jerusalem', *The Horns of Hattin*, ed. B.Z. Kedar, Jerusalem, 1992.

Maalouf, A. *On Identity*, London, 2000.

Maalouf, A. *The Crusades Through Arab Eyes*, Paris, 1983.

Mack, R. *Bazaar to Piazza*, Berkeley, 2002.

Magdalino, P. 'The Medieval Empire (780-1204)', *The Oxford History of Byzantium*, C. Mango, ed., Oxford University Press, 2002.

Magoulias, H J. *Byzantine Christianity: emperor, church, and the West,* Chicago, 1970.

Maguire, E D. 'Ceramic Arts of Everyday Life', in *Glory of Byzantium*, ed. H Evans and W Wixom, New York, 1997.

Maguire, H. 'Images of the Court', in *The Glory of Byzantium*, ed. H Evans and W Wixom, New York, 1997.

Mathews, T. 'Religious Organization and Church Architecture', in *Glory of Byzantium*, ed. H Evans and W Wixom, New York, 1997.

Mathews, T. 'Early Icons of the Holy Monastery of Saint Catherine at Sinai', *Icons from Sinai*, R Nelson and K Collins, eds., Los Angeles, 2006.

Mayer, H E. 'Studies in the History of Queen Melisende of Jerusalem', *Dumbarton Oaks Papers*, 26 (1972), Washington, pp. 95-182.

Mayer, H E. *The Crusades*, 1972.

Metcalf, W. in *The Glory of Byzantium,* ed. H Evans and W Wixom.

Munro, D. 'Urban and the Crusaders', *Translations and Reprints from the Original Sources of European History,* Vol.1:2, Philadelphia 1895.

Nelson, R. 'Where God Walked and Monks Pray', *Icons from Sinai*, R Nelson and K Collins, eds., Los Angeles, 2006 .

Norwich, John Julius. *A Short History of Byzantium*, New York, 1997.

O'Kane, B. *Treasures of Islam*, London, 2007.

Orderic Vitalis. *Ecclesiastical History*, 6.390-93.

Ousterhout, R. 'Secular Architecture', in *The Glory of Byzantium,* ed. H Evans and W Wixom, New York 1997.

Payne, Robert. *The Dream and the Tomb, A History of the Crusades*, New York, 1984.

Perry, C. Foreword in L Zaouali, *Medieval Cuisine of the Islamic World,* Berkeley, 2007.

Petzold, A. *Romanesque Art*, London, 1995.

Phillips, Jonathon. *Holy Warriors, A Modern History of the Crusades*, London, 2009.

Pinder-Wilson, R. 'Islamic Glass, 12th–15th Centuries', *Five Thousand Years of Glass*, ed. H Tait, London 1991, pp. 126-135.

Piponnier, Francoise and Mane, Perrine. *Dress in the Middle Ages*, Paris, 1995.

Prawer, Joshua. *The World of the Crusaders*, New York, 1972.

Raymond of Aguilers. http://www.focusmm.com/civilization/hagia/history.htm.

Riley-Smith, J. *The Atlas of the Crusades*, New York, 1991.

Riley-Smith, J. *The First Crusade and the Idea of Crusading*, New York, 1993.

Riley-Smith, J. *The First Crusaders, 1095-1131,* Cambridge, 1997.

Robert the Monk. *History of the First Crusade*, trans. by Carol Sweetenham, England, 2005.

Rosenwein, Barbara. *A Short History of the Middle Ages*, University of Toronto, 2009.

Runciman, S. *History of the Crusades*, vol. I, Cambridge, 1951.

Runciman, S. *History of the Crusades*, vol. II, Cambridge, 1952 .

Schein, S. 'Women in the Crusader Period', *Knights of the Holy Land*, ed. S Rozenberg, Jerusalem, 1999.

Scott, P. *The Book of Silk*, London, 1993.

Segal, J B. *Edessa 'the blessed city'*, Oxford, Clarendon Press, 1970.

Singman, Jeffrey. *Daily Life in Medieval Europe*, Westport, Ct., 1999.

Soucek, P. 'Byzantium and the Islamic East', in *Glory of Byzantium*, ed. H Evans and W Wixom, New York, 1997.

Soucek, P. 'Artistic Exchange in the Mediterranean Context', in *The Meeting of Two Worlds*, Kalamazoo, 1981.

Stalley, R. *Early Medieval Architecture*, Oxford, 1999 .

Stokstad, M. *Medieval Art*, Boulder, Colorado, 2004.

Thatcher, O, and E H McNeal, eds. *A Source Book for Medieval History*.

Tyerman, Christopher. *God's War, A New History of the Crusades*, Harvard University Press, 2006.

Usamah Ibn-Munqidh. *An Arab-Syrian Gentleman and Warrior in the Period of the Crusades*, trans. P Hitti, New York, 2000.

Vryonis, S. 'Byzantine Society and Civilization' in *The Glory of Byzantium*, ed. H Evans and W Wixom, New York, 1997.

Ward, R. *Islamic Metalwork,* London, 1993.

William of Tyre. *A History*.

Wixom, W. 'Byzantine Art and the Latin West' in *The Glory of Byzatnium,* ed. H Evans and W Wixom, New York, 1997.

Zaouali, L. *Medieval Cuisine of the Islamic World*, Berkeley, 2007.

INDEX